OF ALL EVIL

WILLIAM STYRON'S FICTION

by John Kenny Crane

University of South Carolina Press

Copyright © University of South Carolina 1984
Published in Columbia, South Carolina, by the
University of South Carolina Press

First Edition

Manufactured in the United States of America

Library of Congress Cataloging in Publication Data

Crane, John Kenny, 1942–
   The root of all evil.

   Includes bibliographies.
    1. Styron, William, 1925–   —Criticism and inter-
pretation.   2. Evil in literature. I. Title.
PS3569.T9Z625 1984 813'.54 84–20820
ISBN 0–87249–447–0

For Bev

CONTENTS

ACKNOWLEDGMENTS

I greatly appreciate the advice of three of my colleagues at Penn State: Professor Augustus Kolich, who recognized the Freudian overtones of the concept of Transfer long before I did; Professor Al Miles who admires *Sophie's Choice* somewhat less than I do and showed me where I would have to strengthen my argument to make him listen; and Professor Philip Young who "played hard to get" and shamed me into rewriting the Introduction to this volume more times than I can count. I am indebted to Professor Keen Butterworth of the University of South Carolina and to Professor James L. W. West III of Virginia Polytechnic Institute and State University, who generously lent me their thoughts and reservations as the manuscript entered its final stages. Finally, my thanks to Ms. Kathy Leitzell, no longer a "typist" but now a "processor of words," who stared all those hours at the green screen to produce this manuscript.

—John K. Crane,
The Pennsylvania State University

ABBREVIATIONS

The Root of All Evil

INTRODUCTION

In his 1981 essay "The World in a Mirror: Problems of Distance in Recent American Fiction,"[1] Morris Dickstein takes issue with a number of modern novelists—Philip Roth, Bernard Malamud, John Irving, and William Styron among them—for writing what he calls "confessional" fiction. This fictional form produces novels which "lean so heavily on well-known details of their authors' lives that they amount almost to self-plagiarism."[2] Referring particularly to *Sophie's Choice,* Dickstein says this: "Working with a sliver of experience from his early days as a writer and a mountain of indigestible research on the Holocaust, Styron has no choice but to embellish, and this betrays the book's lack of conviction and formal organization."[3] Most confessional novels, Dickstein concludes, actually "confess very little, and rarely show their authors in a bad light."[4]

While I do not agree with Dickstein in his judgments about Styron's use of the form, I do appreciate that he is among the few to recognize that *Sophie's Choice* is much more about Stingo and his choices than it is about Sophie and hers. A sympathetic critic and historian, Richard L. Rubenstein, has perhaps overstated the matter by calling the novel a *bildungsroman,*[5] but he has insisted as well that the reader realize that the book is more about Stingo's maturation than it is about Sophie's horrifying experiences and her resultant guilt. Rather, Sophie's narrative of Auschwitz is the catalyst for Stingo's coming of age from the brash young writer who dares to open his account of his first summer in New York with a line like "Call me Stingo" to the older Styron who has plumbed the depths of evil in his later novels and has discovered the underlying principle of slavery, Southern or—particularly—German, to be a belief in "the absolute expendability of human life."

Far from being unable to show himself in a bad light as Dickstein has charged, the older Styron is portraying the younger Stingo as having the drive, the desire, the cocksureness to write significant works of fiction but neither the moral awareness nor the sensitivity to do so. As he told one interviewer while he was writing *Sophie's Choice*, "I should emphasize that part of the story is that of a young kid who's desperately yearning to write. He wants to write so bad his teeth ache . . . [but] he has not experienced enough. . . . He has not seen enough of life . . . [to] enable him to apprehend things, to be able to start to write."[6] In the novel itself, young Stingo says "I had the syrup but it wouldn't pour." Later in the novel's opening chapter, he goes on to say that "it was true that I had traveled great distances for one so young, but my spirit had remained landlocked."

The elder Styron is, thus, cajoling, criticizing, satirizing, and even humiliating the younger Stingo in this tale of a young man fighting to unlock his spirit so that he may truly begin to write up to the demands of his inborn literary talent. He shows his young self fighting, and failing, to lose his virginity at all cost; luring the affections of an older woman who loves another man desperately; writing the story of a childhood sweetheart who had recently and conveniently committed suicide at the very moment Stingo needed a story to tell. Stingo funds himself with money his ancestors had gotten by selling an unfortunate slave away from his family on the basis of a false rumor and is able to stifle what little guilt he feels with casual asides, such as "What the hell, once a racist exploiter, always a racist exploiter. Besides, in 1947 I needed $485 as badly as any black man." Still unable to start his pen forward, he imitates and nearly plagiarizes the opening paragraphs of *All the King's Men*, his own rendition standing to this day as the initial pages of Styron's own first novel, *Lie Down in Darkness*.

When Stingo is not shameless, he is desperately naive, imagining himself blissfully married to a woman who does not love him, fathering children who will never exist, living in a home which will resemble Faulkner's, "gaining laurels rarely shed upon the work of a writer so young," farming peanuts on the side, shunning the media in his moody isolation. When his story finally gets itself off the ground and he begins to write it at "runaway speed," he is driven forward by the "tough criticism" of a poseur genius who turns out to be a madman. In an extended passage of self-satire which Styron includes as Stingo and Sophie flee southward from the deranged Nathan, he has Stingo imagine that he will finish his first novel within the next two years (it took four), to have it greeted by reviewers who would find in it "the most powerful passage of female interior monologue since Molly Bloom's." By age thirty, Stingo goes on to presume, he would finish *These Blazing Leaves*, "the chronicle of that tragic Negro firebrand Nat Turner." Not only did Stingo get the title wrong, Stingo-Styron was forty-two before *The Confessions of Nat Turner* was finally completed. "What folly! What conceit!," Stingo laments in retrospect.

By implication, Styron seems to divide his own career into two halves in *Sophie's Choice*. His first three works are either criticized (as *Lie Down in Darkness* was for imitativeness and thematic fuzziness, both by the critics and—here—by Styron), or satirized (*The Long March* is referred to as "a taut, searing book eviscerating the military in a tragicomedy of the absurd"), or forgotten about entirely (there is no mention made at all of *Set This House on Fire*). He is, however, much more defensive about the work of the second half of his career, the work that was produced after he feels himself to have developed into a writer whose vision had focused, whose style had individualized itself, and whose moral awareness had finally grown to match his talent. As the older Styron remarks at the beginning of Chapter Nine of *Sophie's Choice*, "my heart was still with the art of the novel . . . and I was pleased that year of 1967 to be able to disprove its demise (to my personal satisfaction at least) by publishing a work [*The Confessions of Nat Turner*] which,

in addition to fulfilling my own personal and philosophical requirements, as a novelist, found hundreds of thousands of readers—not
all of them, as it turned out later, completely happy about the event."

I believe, therefore, first that *Sophie's Choice* is primarily a story
of Styron becoming an artist rather than a wordsmith. Further, I
contend that an examination of the themes, and more importantly
the thematic unity of *Sophie's Choice*, will reveal the underlying concerns which have compelled Styron to write fiction from the start,
even though, as Katherine Anne Porter has remarked, Styron had
not come to terms with "his own end meanings" because he had
not brought them to the order of true art.[7] Moreover, since Styron
insists in *Sophie's Choice* that he continues to respect *The Confessions
of Nat Turner* above all his other work, I think we can infer that
we should reread that novel and reinterpret it in light of the many
clues about his development as a writer that Styron gives us in his
most recent book. Finally, *Sophie's Choice* can allow us as well to
return to his three earliest works and seek within them the roots
of his as-yet-undeveloped and fuzzily-focused moral vision.

I have organized this study in the same order. I will examine the
themes of *Sophie's Choice* (1979) first and then attempt to demonstrate the ways in which the same themes had already crystallized
for Styron in *The Confessions of Nat Turner* (1967) twelve years
before, even though for one reason or another most, if not all,
critics had failed to recognize them. Next I will turn to his two
pieces of military fiction to contrast his grasp of his central themes
in "Marriott, the Marine" (to have been the opening chapters of
the forthcoming *The Way of the Warrior*) to the narrower conception he had of them in his second work, *The Long March* (1952).
Then I will try to suggest where the seeds of these themes can be
seen beneath the surface of *Lie Down in Darkness* (1951) and *Set
This House on Fire* (1960), his first two full-length novels. Finally
I will conclude with two chapters which consider all the work
together: one on the father-figures who, book after book, attempt
to instill vision in Stingo and other Styron heroes, and the other
on Styron's developing narrative form and the ways in which this
form reveals and emphasizes the themes which emerge most clearly
in *Sophie's Choice*.

Because his art so clearly matured, Styron's later work is by far his most significant. However, because he demonstrates in *Sophie's Choice* exactly how the maturation took place, he has allowed us to return to his first three works and to see them, even though they themselves are not changed, in a different way. Unlike writers who seem to retell the same story over and over again, Hemingway perhaps, Styron has told very distinctly different stories; however, when his earlier work is reconsidered after reading *Sophie's Choice*, the thematic thrust of them emerges as remarkably the same.

Notes

1. *Sewanee Review*, 89 (1981), 386–400.
2. Dickstein, pp. 387–88.
3. Dickstein, p. 387.
4. Dickstein, p. 388.
5. Richard L. Rubenstein, "The South Encounters the Holocaust: William Styron's *Sophie's Choice*," *Michigan Quarterly Review*, 20 (1981), 425–42.
6. Ben Forkner and Gilbert Schricke, "An Interview with William Styron," *The Southern Review*, 10 (1974), p. 923.
7. Cf. George Core, "Nat Turner and the Final Reckoning of Things," *Southern Review*, 4 (1968), p. 747.

1

THE THEMATIC UNITY OF SOPHIE'S CHOICE

" 'I sometimes got to think that everything bad on earth, every evil that was ever invented had to do with my father.' "
—Sophie Zawistowska

While surely these words, spoken by Sophie in a Washington hotel room, are an overstatement, Styron has portrayed in other works, notably *Lie Down in Darkness* and *The Confessions of Nat Turner*, father figures who misdirect their children with visions of the future which are as glorious and orderly as they are highly unlikely. Such indoctrination, Styron seems to be saying in *Sophie's Choice*, can create a lifelong chain of immoral, amoral, and often horrific acts and events which combine to "create" evil on all levels of human experience—anthropological, historical, and personal. Racial and religious prejudice, Nazi extermination camps, and one's own individual suffering all seem to stem from a false vision of human existence which is passed on to each generation by the one which preceded and so reared it. Hence, Sophie's statement, if this contention can be accepted, might not be so ludicrously far-fetched as it at first might seem.

In his densely-plotted and minutely-detailed story, Styron is assembling a vast mosaic of the human race, past and present, in which one fundamental pattern of man-made evil cyclically repeats itself, a pattern to which individuals so apparently diverse as Adolf Hitler and Sophie Zawistowska, Governor Bilbo and Nathan Landau, Sophie's father and even young Stingo subscribe simply because they are human. It is a false vision of reality, but one which is relentlessly passed down from one generation to the next.

Stated as simply as possible, Styron's pattern is this: Each individual is born into his threescore-and-ten a Solitary, his mind a

9

tabula rasa. His outlook is shaped by his parents (though in Styron it is generally the male parent alone), and it usually comprises a set of promises for the future, comfortable visions which suit the parent and so shape the child. That the realization might not finally match the promise is rarely considered, and so the child grows into adulthood expecting the "Parental Plan" to materialize. What is overlooked from the start, however, is the power of Fortune, that irrational, haphazard, and whimsical distributor of limited rewards. Hence, when the promises do not actualize, as most do not, the course of human events seems an aberration to the misguided individual. He feels himself either the only one neglected or, perhaps, the mistreated possessor of special credentials which Fortune has overlooked. Frustrated, he engages in an activity I shall later discuss as "Fortune-forcing" in an attempt to mold men and events according to the original promise, to make his existence reshape itself to the way it "should have been." The fundamental human safeguards against one's baser nature begin to erode; and—depending on the person—virtually anything might become acceptable behavior in an attempt to bring about a "larger purpose" which in the end turns out to be entirely personal and not larger at all. Such apparently dissimilar activities as Nazi genocide, Sophie's willingness to sacrifice others for the safety of herself and her children, and Stingo's libidinal assaults upon anything non-male from Leslie Lapidus to Mary Alice Grimball, all stem from the same fundamental outlook.

The safeguard which Styron seems to recommend as the prevention of such behavior is the ability to experience guilt, the very bugbear modern psychotherapy seems bent upon stripping from the human consciousness. Without a highly developed sense of guilt, any atrocity against one's fellow man might ultimately become, if not right, at least justifiable. Yet, even so, in Styron's universe Fortune will not be forced, or at least not very far. The harder man tries to shove her, the more ironic is his predicament: Hitler a suicide; Sophie's father executed by the very people whose doctrine he held dear; his adored grandchildren swallowed by the amorphous flux of the Third Reich; Stingo mired in a homosexual dream born of his failure to force the unfortunate Mary Alice into bed.

Confronted by the awareness that the promises can never be realized, man turns upon God, blames Him for miscreating the world, proclaims atheism forthwith, turns to painkillers such as drugs (Nathan), booze (Sophie and Stingo), and outright lies (virtually every character in the novel) in an attempt to pretend that things, if they did not go right at the start, have somehow shaped up. In such escapes he remains blinded to the truth, and the whole horrendous chain can now begin again, either in his own generation or in the one that, at the height of his disillusionment, he will spawn.

I would like to examine here the ways in which Styron develops these dimensions of his theme through the people and events, both real and fictional, he weaves into *Sophie's Choice*.[1] Properly understood, the evil portrayed in the novel reveals its own solution. There *is* an answer given, I think, however drunk and crushed Stingo is in the book's final moments. Stingo had a father, too, after all—a good, gentle, articulate, liberal man—who, however slow Stingo is to discern his message, taught quite a different lesson.

The Solitary

If irony is properly defined as a set of circumstances which is the direct opposite of what was expected or considered appropriate, *Sophie's Choice* is a book which presses irony to an extreme. Even the title, which refers to the fact that—on the platform at Auschwitz—Sophie was singled out because she was "not a yid," made special and alone above her fellow man on the train, is loaded with irony. Where the others are to be sent to the crematoriums or the work camp by totalitarian directive, Sophie, the Solitary and special, is given a choice. She can choose which of her children will be exterminated, which will live in bondage. This is the irony and ambiguity in the sense of specialness each of us cultivates for himself or herself from birth.

When the novel opens we view young Stingo, basking in the glorious sunshine of unwritten novels, monomaniacally carving his way through the manuscripts of lesser mortals at McGraw-Hill. He is simply *different* from anyone else, not bound in letter nor spirit to the expectations of his employers, whether they be ridiculous ones such as the proper hat to wear and newspaper to be seen reading or more reasonable ones such as performing his remunerated task rather than floating glue balloons out the window. When he is fired for this, he takes himself out for a "solitary banquet" (*SC*, 27) to celebrate this backhanded recognition that he is different and special. After finding residence in Yetta Zimmerman's Pink Palace, he tries for a time to create a solitude in which this specialness will remain unsullied by the outside world. He shrieks at the ceiling to demand that Sophie and Nathan cease their sexual olympics. When they attempt to initiate friendship by taking him with them to the seashore, he orders them out of his room. Even when he begins to yield to their irresistible attraction, he can still remark to the reader that he is being foolhardy. "I felt this not only because I was afraid of getting sucked toward the epicenter of such a volatile, destructive relationship, but because I had to confront the hard fact that I, Stingo, had other fish to fry . . . 'to write my guts out'."(*SC*, 62) He has not been put on this earth, nor in this city, "to play the hapless supernumerary in some tortured melodrama." (*SC*, 62)

And yet the irony. For all the inclination people have to isolate themselves so that they may realize the future that has been promised them (or in Stingo's case, more appropriately, that he has promised himself), for all their propensity to be alone at the counting table when Fortune dispenses her favors, Styron demonstrates throughout the novel mankind's essential fear of being singled out, its basic disinclination to labor alone and apart from other mortals. Stingo is so drawn to Sophie and Nathan that he often allows his novel to simmer on the back burner while he suns with them on Jones Beach, that he devotes himself to Sophie's anguished stories of the War without any real hope of the sexual consummation he yearns for, that he makes it up with Nathan in an instant despite the most soul-shattering insults and accusations. Later Stingo confesses himself "smitten by the same horror of solitude that causes human beings to get married or join the Rotarians." (*SC*, 112) When it seems as if Sophie will move out of the Pink Palace after her penultimate break-up with Nathan, Stingo feels "crippled, hamstrung" (*SC*, 305) by the potential loss.

This need to be both alone and not alone is manifest in Sophie herself. Free, physically at least, of the terrors of the concentration camps, she arrives in New York terribly alone simply by sheer uprooting. Her first inclination is "to spend the rest of her life avoiding people en masse." (*SC*, 92) She creates for herself a world of few contacts until finally her solitariness and defenselessness lead her into the humiliation from which Nathan saves her. From then on she is entirely vulnerable to Nathan, not only to his love but also to his atrocious maltreatment of her, not only to his sanity but also to his madness. Along the Merritt Parkway in Connecticut she will yield to his demand that she prostrate herself on the ground and allow him to urinate in her mouth, at which point even Nathan fiendishly remarks that she has " 'absolutely no ego at all.' " (*SC*, 340) As she later explains to Stingo, " 'without Nathan I would be . . . nothing.' " (*SC*, 344) This is spoken by the same lady who had earlier tried in every possible way to separate herself from all those around her by refusing to work for the Polish resistance, by claiming to be the lone anti-Semite incarcerated at Auschwitz, and by attempting to seduce Rudolf Höss so that she can obtain favors that would be beyond the comprehension of most of her peers.

Now surely the difference between Stingo and Sophie on this point is that of innocence and experience. Sophie knows things now about life that this man ten years her junior does not. If Sophie discards her solitary identity to perverted extents in this novel—ultimately to a suicide pact which will protect her final union with Nathan—Stingo continues to try to regain his isolation any time his conscious mind considers the matter. He must write, become famous, critically admired, perhaps wealthy. He continually rationalizes, often in terms couched in anti-feminism and anti-Semitism, reasons why he would be better done with Nathan and Sophie and, at other times, with people in general.

It is in the character of Rudolf Höss, and perhaps in his daughter Emmi, that Styron most clearly portrays the dangers of such a specialized view of oneself. " 'I am very conscious,' " Höss once told Sophie, " 'that in many ways I am not like most men of my calling—of men brought up in a military environment. I was never one of the fellows. I have always been aloof. Solitary.' " (*SC*, 281)

A man of discrimination and fine taste, a lover of beauty, he is also both a major theorist behind the "final solution" and the director of a camp where it is carried out. He has lost any sense of relationship or responsibility to his fellow man—even his wife is merely a vessel into which to deposit his seed and Sophie inspires in him much the same reaction. Likewise his daughter, Emmi, surely the only happy little girl in the surrounding several square miles, becomes as a result equally prejudiced and egocentric. Even in so harmless an activity as looking through a photo album, she is incapable of pointing out anyone in those pictures except "me," despite the fact that the pictures are mostly of her swimming "team." Bored as she listens, Sophie begins to notice, "ineluctable as a smotherer's hand, the odor of burning human beings." (*SC*, 399) But Emmi does not—" '*Das bin ich . . . me me me.*' " (*SC*, 398)

Höss is special in his own mind, Emmi in hers, Stingo in his, and, as we shall see, everyone in his or her own. In this sense of solitariness, we have the planting of the seeds of human evil in all Styron's novels.

Fortune

In speaking of Fortune I choose that word over the alternative "Fate" because it connotes something more of *good* luck, of making one's fortune, of being blessed by Fortune than its more ominous substitute does. Good fortune is something the Solitary has either been taught or has imagined he or she will, somewhere, find; and so his or her life becomes a pursuit of it. Styron is suggesting that human beings, first, feel entitled to it and, second, that they will, even if deprived of their expectations, find some way to convince themselves (and others) that they have succeeded nonetheless.

Yet philosophers through the ages have continually insisted that, for any number of reasons, Fortune is fickle; and Styron insists upon this as well. Select virtually any historical metaphor for Fortune and her workings, and the same conclusion must be drawn. The Boethian Wheel of Fortune, for example, is a constantly rotating process in which the person currently blessed would do well to recall that what he or she has is transient and will shortly evaporate. The fellow down on his luck, at the bottom of the wheel so to speak, need only wait till his turn for possessing a measure of luck will spin his way. In addition, the Wheel of Fortune motif suggests that for one person to have *good* fortune, another must have an equal measure of *bad*. There is simply not enough to supply all men at all times. Thus, a tendency might easily set in to try to stop the Wheel, to keep the other down and oneself up.

Sophie's Choice abounds in examples of just this. Sophie and the other Poles on her train arrive at Auschwitz at virtually the same moment that Hitler issues the order that the extermination facilities are henceforth to be used for Jews alone—hence, even in their pitiable state, the Poles are at the top of the Wheel so long as the supply of Jews to fill the crematoriums does not run dry. And there is the lesbian Wilhelmine who can lure the favors of other women because she has access to a supply of silk underpants stolen from slaughtered Jewesses. One's bad fortune is another's good fortune. Or, back home, Mr. Lapidus has invented "the Worm," a shell-detonating device, which has made him rich—had he not had the good fortune to have invented it at a time when America had to resist the destruction of European civilization, he would not have attained the wealth to amass the art treasures which he bought away from those smashed countries.

Another concept of Fortune prevalent, especially in post-Darwinian times, is that of Blind Chance. Styron has incorporated much of this as well. Take, for example, the poor swan Tadeusz, "a small male considerably less agile and scruffier than the others" (*SC*, 135) whom Sophie feeds on her outings to Prospect Park. This is Darwinian natural selection on one level, blind chance, though it is also blind chance that the poor creature has the likes of Sophie come along who will direct her offerings in his direction to make sure "that he got more than his share of the garbage." (*SC*, 136) Another example is Dr. Blackstock, Sophie's benevolent employer, who, Stingo says, "was one of God's blessed whose destiny had led him from the stony poverty of a *shtetl* in Russian Poland to the most sublime satisfactions that American materialistic success could offer." (*SC*, 96) Equally guided by blind chance is unexpected bad fortune, such as, to use the same character as an example, Blackstock's loss of his beloved wife, decapitated in a boozy car wreck on the Triborough Bridge. His mainstay gone, Blackstock is suddenly no longer one of God's blessed and is on the verge of suicide before Sophie and others manage to pull him through.

Fortune is portrayed through a number of other traditional metaphors as well, but I would like to cite just one. There is that curious undirected interlocking of human wills which Robert Penn Warren called "the Great Twitch," and which another of Styron's influences, William Faulkner, likened, via Judith Sutpen, to "five or six people all trying to weave a rug on the same loom,"[2] each to his or her own design. Philosophically this has often gone under the label of the Schopenhauerian "Will-Web" where each of us, no matter how virtuous, simply manages to get in the way of, and so impede and perhaps destroy, innocently but thoroughly, the designs of others. In the book's most memorable scene, if Stingo's interpretation is correct, Dr. Von Niemand simply had had enough of blind slaughter which had failed to cause him the twitch of a moral eyelash. And so, in a supreme effort to make himself feel guilt once again by doing the most horrendous thing his liquor-soaked mind could conceive of, he forced Sophie to make the choice of which of her two young children she will send to the extermination chamber. His new design has therewith saddled Sophie with a guilt she will never fully shed. Or there is Feldshon, the Jewish underground leader who depends upon Sophie's friend Lotte to supply him with firearms, who feels betrayed by the designs of others when she can produce only three pistols—" 'We are being left to drown by our countrymen!' " (*SC*, 472) Likewise, however, the will-web can occasionally bring someone else accidental *good* fortune, such as Bronek who catches Höss's fancy perhaps only by "the language he spoke, the droll garbled German of an uneducated Pole from Pomerania" (*SC*, 258) and so is moved into the protection of the Commandant's house.

Styron demonstrates, then, the irony of expecting to regulate Fortune when, whatever the metaphor, it is so essentially beyond anyone's control. Yet, man's self-respect and the admiration of others seem to stem entirely from at least *appearing* to control events and circumstances, and pecking orders are instantly established in all societies in order to evaluate one's ability—even in concentration camps. Sophie, for example, is given a "more favored position than many of the other prisoners" (*SC*, 145) because of her knowledge of German and Russian. Because she is the right age and in good health she is sent to Auschwitz to work instead of into the crematoriums to die. Given the limitations of her situation, she is high on Fortune's pecking order, one of the "chosen."

The novel is scattered with such blindly ironic estimations of one's own rank on Fortune's scale. The librarian who causes Sophie's collapse outranks her simply because he knows that there is no American poet named Dickens and Sophie does not. Stingo, having failed miserably in his attempts to seduce loose-mouthed, tightly-corseted Leslie Lapidus, actually moves himself up his own pecking order: ". . . in compensation, I reasoned, I had more exalted goals. After all, I was a writer, an artist, and it was a platitude by now that much of the world's great art had been achieved by dedicated men who, husbanding their energies, had not allowed some misplaced notion of the primacy of the groin to subvert grander aims of beauty and truth." (*SC*, 179) In a parallel situation at Auschwitz, two middle-aged Jewish sisters, dressmakers, are spared the collective fate of their race because of "their energetic yet delicate artistry with needle and thread," all day long refurbishing for Höss's women "much of the fancier clothing taken from Jews who had gone to the gas chambers." (*SC*, 254)

And so, in a world in which Fortune haphazardly doles out her expected rewards, Stingo, Sophie, and Nathan clamber blindly for their share. Because of the ill-treatment of the slave Artiste in the last century, Stingo suddenly receives a $500 legacy which will allow him to remain jobless all summer. (Until, that is, Fortune turns on him, and he has it stolen from his band-aid box.) The sad news of the suicide of his adolescent sex goddess, Maria Hunt, can be turned, with the stroke of a pen, into the subject of Stingo's first novel, one which brought him fame and, trite though it sounds, fortune. Farrell's son was killed on Okinawa and Jack Brown lost part of a leg on Iwo Jima while Stingo, by lucky accident of birth, failed to get to the Pacific before the war ended. "Fortune's darling" (*SC*, 24) he labels himself early on.

Less fortunate is Sophie who found her idyllic childhood erased by the horrors of the Holocaust. If her safety at Auschwitz was assured by the abundant supply of Jews to die in her place, most of the rest of Fortune's doles are horrid indeed. The simple act of stealing a ham for her tubercular mother lands her at Auschwitz, a fate she might otherwise have avoided. Moreover, it is such foul use at the hands of Fortune which drives Nathan to madness. A Jew blessed to live in the United States at the time his people were being indiscriminately destroyed, he cannot accept the fact that he was so cleanly spared. He tries to make amends, ironic in itself, by caring for Sophie, by lending Stingo money when his is lost to a Brooklyn catburglar, by imagining himself curing cancer for all mankind. But ultimately he goes mad, blaming Sophie for her sheer failure to die with the others and dragging her with him, as a consequence, into suicide.

That Nathan is Sophie's "savior . . . but her destroyer as well" (*SC*, 136), that Sophie and Wanda meet the same fate despite the fact that Sophie had stayed entirely clear of Wanda's subversive activities, that Governor Bilbo dies of tongue cancer after having used that organ to consolidate his political base through "promiscuous public use of words like 'nigger,' 'coon,' 'jigaboo' " (*SC*, 189)—all these are the ironies of uncontrolled and uncontrollable Fortune. Evil will result, however, when the individual, unable to tolerate these ironies, will not admit that they exist and so continues to try to shape Fortune to his or her own conception of how it should behave.

Promise/Realization

" 'Consider, Sophielove,' " [Nathan] was saying now, caressing the two [cyanide] capsules, " 'consider how intimately life and death are intertwined in Nature, which contains everywhere the seeds of our beatitude and our dissolution.' " (*SC*, 332)

Depressing as such an understanding might be, deterministic in the extreme, Styron seems to suggest that mankind's sheer failure to acknowledge this fact results in its futile attempts to manipulate Fortune. This is not to say that Nathan's recognition of it and his attendant suicide to hurry the process is the proper way to do so. Nor, of course, are Nazi extermination camps which underscore much the same metaphysical reality. Yet this very admission on mankind's part could, if properly treated, provide it with an explanation of why Fortune and its fruits ripen (if they do) only to decay (which they must). It is simply Nature's pattern, a fact of life.

Unfortunately each individual tries to resist this at all costs, simply because from his or her youth he or she is provided with promises which will "surely" be realized. Sophie many times discusses her beautiful childhood and even the close moments she shared then with her father. She cannot, of course, reconcile them with the debacle of the concentration camp into which her young adulthood materialized and the savage anti-Semite her father proved to be. In Sophie's case this is just an extreme manifestation of a predictable natural pattern in Styron's novel.

Once again Styron's complex and dense writing surrounds the three main characters with almost uncountable examples of this on every imaginable level. Farrell failed both to become a writer and to live the writer's life vicariously through his son. Other aspiring writers ship their manuscripts to McGraw-Hill to have them vandalized by young Stingo and his ilk. Governor Bilbo, who, in his early years, had "produced reforms and contributions that had greatly advanced the common weal" (*SC*, 190), later became the despicable red-necked bigot in whose death Stingo finds justice and Nathan pleasure. Or there is Dürrfeld, the magnetic, masculine industrialist whom Sophie sexually craves when he visits her father but who, when she sees him again at Auschwitz, has become an inhuman devourer of Jewish labor, committed to sapping the last ounce of strength from their doomed bodies. And we cannot overlook the German doctor Stingo dubs Von Niemand, in training for the ministry as a youth, later a drunken lout whose duty it became to separate the fit from the unfit on the platform at Auschwitz.

Even places are demonstrated to travel the same course. The nineteenth-century Germany Sophie's father believes himself to be preserving has long since given way to the Third Reich and its stormtroopers. As he leaves New York on the train south with Sophie, Stingo ruefully observes "New Jersey's satanic industrial barrens" and wonders what "Thomas Jefferson [would] have thought, viewing this?" (*SC*, 451) Northern Virginia has become so urbanized that, late in the book, Stingo does not even recognize it and vows never again, if possible, to go there. Promise and realization. There is some law of decay which seems virtually irresistible and therefore terribly disillusioning. Even the Maple Court, the sleazy bar in which Sophie tells much of her story to Stingo, had been built to be a grand dance palace which the neighborhood after the fact rejected.

If this principle of realization never equaling the promise can be endured on impersonal and categorical levels, it cannot be within the framework of one's own life. The stakes are higher here. For Stingo the grand promises of Leslie Lapidus yield only a tortured mind and an aching groin and a vow to live, henceforth, a monkish existence. Later, Mary Alice Grimball, a talented masturbator of her boyfriends, drives him to his first homosexual dream as a result. In terms of his chosen profession, Styron-Stingo has been lured by the "grand certitude" of Thomas Wolfe—"the certitude that the well-springs of youth would never run dry, and that the wrenching anguish endured in the crucible of art would find its recompense in everlasting fame, and the love of beautiful women." (*SC*, 198) When, near the end of the story, Sophie and Nathan seem to have suffered their final break from one another, Stingo imagines an idealized life on Hobbs' vacant peanut farm, the blacks planting and reaping, he writing, she mothering, their children sporting Polish names and American futures. As if to underscore that things are in fact going according to plan, Stingo finds warmth in the "Southern" reception they get as the Reverend Entwistle and his wife at the Washington hotel. And then of course follows the night of passionate sex in which Stingo feels they "came close [to doing] . . . everything it is possible to do." (*SC*, 496) He falls asleep, happily exhausted, but wakes to find her gone for good and, within hours, dead by her own hand. Promise and realization. They do not jibe in *Sophie's Choice*.

It is an understatement to say, of course, that they do not in Sophie's life either. If she has already lowered her sights by the time she first encounters Stingo, they were once set as high as his. She recalls a photograph her father took of her at thirteen, she and her mother sitting at the piano playing a composition for four hands, totally happy, Sophie undoubtedly anticipating her future as a pianist and a piano teacher. Now in 1947, she can simply recall the picture, now lost, as " 'a symbol of what was and could have been and now cannot be.' " (*SC*, 142) With the loss of her father and husband at the beginning of the war, the original promises are lost; but, again true to man's propensity to seek some sort of realization of Fortune's promise nonetheless, she simply alters the means she will use for making at least *some* promises pay off despite it all.

Once again it is a matter of altering the terms of one's expectations. The fact that her musical career is not to come about must, obviously, be accepted once she has been incarcerated at Auschwitz. But a new form of the same sort of thinking replaces it. Noting the special role she has because of such lucky accidents as her linguistic abilities and the Nazis' current need for them, she presumes that she can increase her stature still further. At one point or another she believes that she can free herself (though not anyone else) by displaying her father's anti-Semitic pamphlet to Höss. Or by seducing him, with her body if she must, she can gain access to her child, she can have him placed in the Lebensborn program, or perhaps she can gain various other favors that Höss's libido might grant her. None of this works, of course—promise and realization again—and Höss castigates her for her open attempts to influence him. He is eventually transferred back to Berlin, leaving Sophie with none of the promises she had depended upon.

Much the same thing happens to her in Brooklyn. At one point she calls Nathan her savior. Stingo calls him her "Prince Charming." Yet Nathan is mad, carries cyanide capsules in his pocket, and will eventually destroy her. In another example, they take a weekend trip to Connecticut for relaxation, and before it is over Sophie has been accused of selling her body to Nazis to get out of Auschwitz, has been aligned with Irma Griese in her supposed anti-Semitism, and nearly does not return from the trip alive. Small relaxation!

If anything, Nathan once again is all too aware that the collapse of promise has not occurred in his life to an extent to make him worthy in his own mind of association with his fellow man. Though mad to a degree we are never quite sure of, he still has a satisfactory job, a large group of friends, money, a devoted brother, and the ability to inspire love in both Sophie and Stingo. It is characteristic of Nathan, then, that he *knows* many of the lessons that the others do not about promise and its unlikely realization; so he attempts to shape his own destiny to underscore them and thus make him worthy to exist in this misbegotten world for so long as he chooses to.

Fortune-Forcing

Most of the other characters, however, try to compel events in the opposite direction. With Fortune inexplicably against them, with promises unrealized, they commence attempting to remind Fortune of its duties toward them. They try to force events to travel in directions which are unnatural. The Southern misuse of an entire race of people lingers in the background as an example of Fortune-forcing on a racial, perhaps cosmic level. In the foreground, obviously, so is the Nazi attempt to rid the universe of the Jewish race. Styron accepts these as the givens of history and demonstrates that these cataclysmic inhumanities are results of millions of individual inclinations in the same direction.

Styron, as he always does in this book, attempts to underscore his thesis with examples that range from the mundane and insignificant to the tragic and appalling. When the Weasel takes over at McGraw-Hill, he attempts to reform his employees—particularly Stingo—with regard to dress and reading habits. In the opposite direction, Rudolf Höss recognizes that " ' . . . the prisoners never missed an opportunity for doing some little act of kindness to my wife or children, and thus attracting their attention.' " (*SC*, 154) More bluntly stated is Lotte's version of the same *modus operandi*: " 'Kiss [Wilhelmine's] ass . . . lick her ass good and you won't have no trouble.' " (*SC*, 255) The Lebensborn program is a form of Fortune-forcing as well, as are the chaotic reactions of the citizens of Warsaw on the train which is carrying them to Auschwitz and Birkenau:

> . . . two frightened convent girls of sixteen or so, sobbing, sleeping, waking to murmur prayers to the Holy Virgin; Wiktor, a black-haired, intense, infuriated young Home Army member already plot-

ting revolt or escape, ceaselessly scribbling messages on slips of paper to be passed to Wanda in another compartment; a fear-maddened shriveled old lady claiming to be the niece of Wieniawski, claiming the bundle of parchment she kept pressed close to her to be the original manuscript of his famous *Polonaise,* claiming some kind of immunity, dissolving into tears like the schoolgirls at Wiktor's snarled remark that the Nazis would wipe their asses on the worthless *Polonaise.*" *(SC,* 479)

And of course Sophie has her anti-Semitic pamphlet tucked in her boot for later use. However understandable these actions are in most cases, forgivable in many, despicable in still others, they all represent instinctive attempts to force Fortune back onto its "promised" track. Such efforts are usually made by individuals for themselves, as here, but they can also be group-oriented. For example, the prisoners, packed tightly into the death train, had initially congratulated themselves that since they had been shoved into a lush tourist coach instead of a boxcar they would be better treated.

Since young Stingo sees himself as "Fortune's darling," he perhaps needs to do less Fortune-forcing than the others—so far. But he is sexually frustrated, and we see him trying to force a change in his fortunes with the prostitute with whom he fails, with Leslie Lapidus (the repressed), and with Mary Alice Grimball (the misused and abandoned). Early in the book we see him writing false jacket blurbs to sell worthless books, and a few pages later we observe him instigating a slow-down strike to resist the Weasel's policies. Later he reveals that he had gorged himself on bananas to make the lower weight limit for the Marine Corps. He sweeps Sophie out of town and onto a train for the farm where they will raise the children he has already assigned names to if not fathered, and he plans the order of his career (in retrospect all backwards and mistitled). In the last moments he spends with Sophie he becomes aware for the first time of the folly of Fortune-forcing, at least with regard to her: "And I suddenly grasped another truth: how ludicrous it was of me to think of a wedding and sweet uxorious years down on the old plantation when the mistress of my passion . . . was lugging around with her wedding clothes meant to please a man she had loved to the point of death. Christ, my stupidity!" *(SC,* 492)

A number of the matters I discussed in other contexts with regard to Sophie could be understood as Fortune-forcing as well—her steering her leftovers toward the swan Tadeusz or her attempts to seduce Höss, for example. In contrast to Stingo, however, Sophie's tries at Fortune-forcing are more plentiful, more instinctive, perhaps more justified, though no less futile. In working for Höss, for instance, she was actually an "accessory—however haphazard and ambiguous and uncalculating her design—to the mass slaughter . . . of Birkenau." (*SC*, 214) In another context she even says she would do anything from licking Nazi boots to killing a Pole or a Jew in order to see her son. Severely disillusioned by Christianity, she lies to Von Niemand that she is a believer. Despite their dissimilarities of dimension, these are all attempts to set Fortune straight. Often they are performed, as is the case with so much that relates to Fortune, at the expense of someone else—Sophie will abandon Wanda and her colleagues in order to keep her own nose clean just as the Nazis will exterminate Jews to purify their race.

It would be unfair not to note perhaps that there is another group of activities in this book which might be termed Fortune-forcing as well. I mean such things as Wanda's underground army to resist the Nazi takeover, Sophie's attempt to steal Emmi's radio to bring the outside world to the waiting inmates, and the like. While I would not want to argue the matter, these might be seen, instead, as attempts to let Fortune restore itself to its natural course which, one at least hopes, was *not* to have been the final elimination of Jews, Poles, Catholics, gypsies, or all those races the 1970s Stingo discovers to have been Hitler's targeted.

Finally there is Nathan. Suicide and attendant pacts are surely Fortune-forcing devices. But note as well the form his delusions take. Each of his experiments is designed to lessen the physical pain of mankind, even to the cure of polio. Noble motives, compelled by a tortured heart; but, at least for Nathan, doomed to failure.

Guilt

A critical catch phrase which has caught favor among Styron's reviewers is that, as a writer, he seeks no less than to discover the source of evil.[3] To whatever extent he has, at this point in his career, found it, I believe it to be located in the next aspect of *Sophie's Choice* that I will consider. As the ironies of Fortune are exposed and misunderstood, as promises are not realized, as attempts to give Fortune a push or a kick prove useless, the human heart becomes hardened. It begins to isolate itself in a tacit belief that only oneself has been so treated, and the ability to feel guilt for one's actions is diminished. To my mind the root of all evil in Styron's universe is the inability to feel guilt for one's actions. For Styron, I think, modernity is getting ever worse, hence more evil, in this matter. Leslie Lapidus and her avant-garde group on the beach who speak so broadly of their psychoanalyses are all about the process of "shedding" guilt. For Styron it would be more appropriate to begin restoring much of what we have lost.

Styron underscores this point at his own cost from the book's earliest pages. There we see young Stingo, twenty-two, aspiring writer reading the hard-if-not-well-wrought work of others "with the magisterial, abstract loathing of an ape plucking vermin from his pelt." (*SC*, 5) Since I believe Stingo to be the central character of *Sophie's Choice* and not Sophie, I believe the novel's main thematic thrust to be Stingo's progressive learning of both guilt and the correspondent inability to commit or allow the sort of evil which left his sickly mother in an unheated room in his boyhood, tortured writers' souls on the junkheap in his young adulthood, and perhaps races of people—Jews, Negroes, Irishmen, or whoever might get in his way—the victims of his pen in his middle age.

Once again Styron places Stingo in a world in which such lack of guilt is the norm rather than the exception. The calumnies of the aptly named Morris Fink cause all sorts of difficulty early in the book for the jealous Nathan and the defenseless Sophie. An unknown hand on a darkened subway car seizes the opportunity to explore Sophie's vagina. Even the inmates at Auschwitz serve the sole function of keeping the crematoriums at Birkenau in operation. Over and over Styron gives us portraits of people—real and fictional—who cause great evil due to their inability to feel remorse or sympathy toward their victims. The cultured, disciplined, in other ways humane Rudolf Höss can not only operate the crematoriums but also forbid his children to mention it in the house so no reflection need be done on the matter.

Now Stingo, to this point in his young life, has not been victimized by this attitude in others, but surely Sophie has. Yet she still is able—not only before Auschwitz but during and after it as well—to repeatedly demonstrate this same, for Styron cataclysmic, shortcoming in herself. In the years before the Nazi horror touched her and her own family, Sophie, if not patently anti-Semitic, was able to type her father's fascist pamphlets and distribute them on command. Since her feeling for the Jews he was attempting to victimize was at best "indifference," his bestowal upon her of "small rewards . . . caused Sophie to accept without any conscious resentment his complete domination of her life." (*SC*, 241) In being blessed by Fortune she at her typewriter resembles Stingo at his pad of rejection slips.

Even after her good Fortune has long since ceased, the inability to feel the sort of guilt Styron suggests might be the best cure for evil persists unabated. She absolutely refuses to work for the Polish underground, even when she alone among them can command the German language. Although she can cite her maternal instincts as being the cause of her reluctance to participate in the salvation of her countrymen, she is able to believe for a long period of time that "the mere presence of the Jews, and the preoccupation the Nazis had with their extermination, would somehow benefit her own security. And the safety of Jan and Eva." (*SC*, 478)

Once "softly" placed above her fellows in Höss's house, she is able to harden her heart against the well-being of others to secure her own continued safety. Even worse than what she had done for her father, she is able not just to type for Höss but also to articulate his phrases better than he can and so become his "accomplice." (*SC*, 219) In order not to upset things for herself (and perhaps for Jan, about whose fate she is always in doubt), she is able to place herself "beyond revulsion" (*SC*, 263) and allow the brutish Wilhelmine to lingually rape her. In virtually every category, words and deeds that would have appalled her when she was more blessed by Fortune become "fleeting commonplaces" (*SC*, 226) in an environment in which Fortune has shortchanged her and so must be manipulated—forced—no matter what the expense to others, themselves equally misused.

Even afterward, safe now in Brooklyn, she is able to utter anti-Semitic remarks about Nathan and random other Jews as if she had not been rescued by three of them—Nathan, Blackstock, and Larry Landau—and as if she had not for many months faced the same dreadful fate as they did for the same abstracted reasons. If Sophie is a valid case in point, no matter how blessed nor how defiled man is, always he is able to place himself first in the search for rewards and favors which, if the theories of Fortune I have discussed are accurate, must ultimately be gotten at the expense of someone else. The individual is always able to convince himself or herself that what he or she has is not enough, that he or she alone has been shortchanged, and that no guilt need be felt as a consequence of anything he or she will do to correct that. Hence, individual men and women manufacture Evil.

Nathan, though on the surface a different sort, is actually much the same. It is true that he does feel an enormous amount of guilt at having evaded the Holocaust, and this guilt takes positive shape in his favors for Sophie and his broadening concern for victimized minorities such as Southern Negroes. But, in being overblessed by Fortune, Nathan can also turn on himself and others whom he perceives to have been equally favored—whether they be rich chiropractors, Southern whites, or even a Polish Catholic girl who had the good luck to get out of the concentration camps alive. Nathan demands that all such make amends. In a certain sense this is not much different from the behavior of Stingo, Sophie, and others that I have been discussing: he has a mental vision of how Fortune should have behaved, will now attempt to force it into shape, and so can leave hotelkeepers' dinners to burn, an aspiring writer's manuscript figuratively in shreds, and his beloved continually anticipating a cyanide capsule.

No theme in *Sophie's Choice* is, I think, pressed harder than this one, for Styron virtually litters his pages with cameos of people possess this same fatal human failing. There is the cabbie who insults

Stingo's father's dignity over the matter of a tip. Princess Czarto-ryska who visits Sophie's father to manufacture hatred against the Jews while they listen to Lieder. The sycophantic Polish contractor who bewails his inability to transport gravel to the crematoriums fast enough. Even the Jews "posed as the only people worthy of salvation" (*SC*, 275), and thus, according to Sophie, are getting what they deserve. A Nazi guard strips the clothes off a nun and has his dog attack her. And there are Bilbo and Von Niemand.

This inability to feel guilt, whether it be on monumental levels or on lesser ones, all reflects some dimension of what Stingo attributes the ability of the Nazis to build extermination camps to: "the simple but absolute *expendability* of human life." (*SC*, 235)

Yet not everyone succumbs to this instinct, and ultimately that will be the factor to which Styron will turn to seek a reversal of this destructive process and the answer to the question Sophie herself asks, midway through the novel: " 'Why this man would allow himself to become a vicious Kapo, who would be cruel to his fellow prisoners and cause many of them to die. Or why this other man or woman would do this or that brave thing, sometime lose their lives that another could live.' " (*SC*, 286)

God

Before turning to Styron's answers to that question, I would like to examine two further factors in the chain of reasoning I have been following. The first is Styron's consideration, on the surface all too standard, of the role of God in what might be termed more a "divine mistake" than a Divine Plan.

Many of the usual outcries of modern agnosticism are present in the book. Perhaps the first note sounded is the "inhumanity" of a God who would take Farrell's son in the bud of his youth. Then of course will follow the oft-asked questions about God's role in allowing the extermination camps to exist in the first place and permitting Evil to run loose in the universe even before that. The name of God and the name of Hitler will be invoked together on the same sampler in Emmi Höss's room, and the middle-aged Stingo will go so far late in the novel as to say "I hate the Judeo-Christian

God." (*SC*, 379) While listening to Sophie's final revelation about Von Niemand, young Stingo invokes the name of God over and over, though for him it is little more than frustrated cussing, "that [was] whispered again and again [and was] as empty as any idiot's dream of God, or the idea that there could be such a Thing." (*SC*, 466) The "believers" he portrays as bombastic or happily unquestioning—the Reverend DeWitt, say, who delivers the homily at Sophie's and Nathan's funeral or the black woman on the bus up from Washington who fondles her bible even as the desperate Stingo does his own.

Yet the very fact that Styron has placed the black religious experience at the penultimate point in his novel, much as he does in *Lie Down in Darkness*, should provide at least a small clue that he is not willing to travel the easy road on the subject that, say, post-War cant might have him do. Rather the novel seems to suggest that, in man's frustration at not having the promise realized, he is willing finally to turn on God and demand that He either take the blame for what went wrong or at least admit that He never existed in the first place. There is need for a scapegoat for all this, and God—at least for Stingo and Sophie—does quite nicely.

If my contention can be accepted that Sophie, for all the liking we usually have and the sympathy we always feel for her, is as flawed a human being as virtually anyone else in the tale, then it is unlikely that Styron would allow her to articulate his story's position on the subject of God. When she chases off mendicant nuns because they are God's earthly representatives, when she nearly commits suicide in a Swedish church to teach Him a lesson, when she imagines having sex with Dürrfeld on an altar, when she tells Höss—for gain, once again—that she " 'abandoned that pathetic faith [Catholicism]' " (*SC*, 275), she is quite clearly trying to pay back what she feels she has unfairly received. She cannot even listen to Handel, and she buys a diaphragm to symbolize her final rejection of God and Catholicism.

But she has doubts as well, and it is these that Styron prefers to explore. " 'I don't know any more, about *when* God leave me. Or I left Him.' " (*SC*, 232) This confusion, expressed to Stingo in the earlier stages of their relationship, is meaningful. The latter sentence suggests Sophie in control, abandoning the deity in disgust. The former suggests exactly the reverse, that God in disgust abandoned her—and mankind. Though Styron does not develop this theme as thoroughly as might be expected, it does seem to me that he makes his position on who abandoned whom rather clear by the end of the book. If "Fuck God" is the last we hear from Sophie on the subject (*SC*, 500), it is not the last from Stingo. Walking on Coney Island beach after the funeral, he reflects on the familiar query " 'At Auschwitz, tell me, where was God?' " and imagines the answer " 'Where was man?' "(*SC*, 513)

This is precisely the point. Man was off in pursuit of the realization of the promises of Fortune, proceeding now to use others to attain what he has so far been deprived of. Auschwitz was simply the most extreme manifestation of the most banal of human weaknesses. The fault here is not God's—unless we wish to suggest that He should have done something about the peculiar workings of the Wheel of Fortune in the first place. The fault is man's.

But, as I would now like to demonstrate, man has yet one more way to exacerbate the horror of the life he has made for himself.

Lying

". . . Sophie told me a number of lies that summer. Perhaps I should say she indulged in certain evasions which at the time were necessary in order for her to retain her composure." (*SC*, 97)

So says Stingo, openly, but I think Styron is demonstrating throughout *Sophie's Choice* that, given the collapse of one's promises and the failure of Fortune, lying to oneself and to others becomes the last resort in at least *pretending* that life did in fact finally take shape. But, as Stingo writes at another moment, lies serve a secondary function as well:

> . . . Sophie was not quite straightforward in her recital of past events. . . . in the long run there may have been multiple reasons, but the word "guilt," I discovered that summer, was often dominant in her vocabulary, and it is now clear to me that a hideous sense of guilt always chiefly governed the reassessments she was forced to make of her past. (*SC*, 146–47)

Lies, in other words, temper or eliminate the sense of guilt one might still have lingering for the actions he or she has taken to wrest Fortune's prize from her recalcitrant grip. Styron again shows character after character lying in countless different ways either to fool themselves or others or to eliminate torturous guilt. In the long run, however, Stingo-Styron seems rather to prefer the refusal to lie that André Gide demonstrates in his journals:

> I won't dwell on this passage here, except to note my admiration therein not only for the terrible humiliations Gide had been able to absorb, but the brave honesty with which he seemed always determined to record them: the more catastrophic the humiliation or the disappointment, I noted, the more cleansing and luminous became Gide's account in his *Journals*—a catharsis in which the reader, too, could participate. (*SC*, 172–73)

The lies perpetrated by various characters in this novel are so inventive that they ultimately defy classification, but they appear to fall into three broad categories. First, there are those which are simply fundamental conscious attempts to make facts seem other than they are. Among these would be simple untruths, such as Sophie's claim that Nathan is the only man other than her husband she ever made love to; her omission that she had two children, not one, at Auschwitz; or her attempt to justify Nathan's drugged speeding to a Connecticut policeman by saying that his mother was dying in Boston. Another of this sort might be called "purposeful ignorance," the refusal to learn the truth when it is readily available. Morris Fink, for example, never answers telephones for fear of what he will hear. Sophie retires to Höss's basement so she will not have to think about the smell of burning human flesh, and later she closes her eyes almost totally so she will not have to view the newsreels of war-torn Europe. Another sort of lying that falls into this category is, I think, active denial of a truth another holds when it does not suit one's purposes. Nathan is perhaps the most adept at this in his constant refusal, at the height of his rages, to accept that Sophie is not sleeping with Katz, Blackstock, or Stingo and that she did not have sex with Höss and every other Nazi at Auschwitz to gain favors. Last in this group is "simple self-delusion," such as believing oneself headed for better things because transported to the crematoriums in a tourist car rather than a boxcar, Sophie's uncle claiming that the Polish troops can defeat the invading Germans because they know the terrain, or Stingo's euphoria about returning to the South which makes him forget "blowflies, . . . underpaid darkies, . . . [and] pig shit" (*SC*, 492) in the Tidewater.

The second category of lies are those which dull the mind so that truth cannot be felt or comprehended. Sophie is virtually an alcoholic by the time of her death. Nathan is a drug addict. The triumvirate goes to Coney Island to experience "visceral glee" on the leftover World's Fair rides. Höss busies himself with a manual on septic tanks which allows him to repress his camp's other business. Stingo tells Sophie Southern jokes to make her forget her troubles as they flee from Nathan. If no such methods work, there is always "sleep [which] allowed the only sure escape from ever-abiding torment." (*SC*, 254) Despite their apparent dissimilarity, all of these activities are ways in which the mind can be deadened to the reception of truth.

I think sex fits this second category as well, especially as indulged in by Sophie and Nathan. While Stingo, in his early attempts to get beyond its decibels, presumes this is simple animal lust, he later, with Sophie in bed with him, revises his opinion, understanding now that sex, for her, "was a frantic and orgiastic attempt to beat back death." (*SC*, 496) Even Höss, in his refusal to yield to Sophie's advances, admits that he would like to have intercourse with her because it " ' "would allow me to lose myself, I might find forgetfulness." ' " (*SC*, 282)

The third category of lying incorporates all those activities that attempt to rewrite reality in a different form, as opposed to denying it (the first category) or blinding oneself to it (the second). Prevalent in this group are dreams which various of the characters have. Stingo, after his failure with Leslie Lapidus, falls into a compensatory dream that he did in fact ultimately fondle one breast, "soggy ball of dough" (*SC*, 178) though it was. In prison camp Sophie dreams of "averted evil, of safety, of answered prayer and jubilant resurrection." (*SC*, 256) Stingo even brings Maria Hunt back to life in a dream, totally changed, "standing before me, with the abandon of a strumpet stripping down to the flesh—she who had never removed in my presence so much as her bobbysocks." (*SC*,

45) Although a number of dreams have the reverse effect—such as Sophie's frightening vision of Czartoryska or Stingo's final nightmare on the Coney Island beach, "a compendium of all the tales of Edgar Allan Poe" (*SC*, 515)—dreams are denials of reality as it is.

So are fantasies. Horny young Stingo fantasizes on the "real" life of the Winston Hunnicutts next door. Sophie and Dürrfeld fantasize about the happy times they might have together in Bayreuth. Perhaps some of the saddest fantasies are those Stingo has late in the novel about his future life as a husband, father, writer, and Southern gentleman with Sophie by his side.

Other sorts of lies which seem to fit this category are such things as Stingo and Sophie assuming the identities of the Reverend and Mrs. Entwistle to register in the Hotel Congress; Nathan's and Sophie's fancy dress costumes which allow them to pretend they live in another place and another time; and even Farrell's plan to live out his dream to be an author vicariously through his son.

If religion has failed as a way to demand that God repay us for our good behavior and redirect the course of time, history, and—especially—Fortune in our favor, the lie, in whatever category, pretends that it has been done nonetheless. It allows us to deny reality and remain atop the Wheel of Fortune even at the moment that same wheel is actually making grist of us. Sophie and Nathan die in an eternal embrace which is as pathetic in the symbolic value they had attached to it as it is in the actuality of two ruined lives.

Transfer

What then do we do? Better still, according to Styron, what should man have been doing all along to lessen the horror of the existence his novel portrays?

We come then finally to what I will refer to as Styron's theory of Transfer. Quoting Hannah Arendt, Styron-Stingo focuses on the problem of lack of guilt I discussed earlier, the passage itself setting up the possibility for what I call "Transfer." Writing of those who actually operated the extermination chambers, Arendt says:

> "The problem was not so much how to overcome their conscience as the animal pity by which all normal men are affected in the presence

of physical suffering. The trick used . . . was very simple and probably very effective; it consisted in turning those instincts around, as it were, in directing them toward the self. So that instead of saying: What horrible things I did to people!, the murderers would be able to say: What horrible things I had to watch in the pursuance of my duties, how heavily the task weighed upon my shoulders!" (*SC*, 153)

The "turning around" that Arendt speaks of is a pivot in the wrong direction, away from "Transfer" rather than toward it. Transfer, rather, is better represented in this quotation Stingo takes, at another point in the story, from George Steiner dealing with what Steiner calls "time relation." Discussing the deaths of two Jews at Treblinka, Steiner writes:

"Precisely at the same hour in which Mehring and Langner were being done to death, the overwhelming plurality of human beings, two miles away on the Polish farms, five thousand miles away in New York, were sleeping or eating or going to a film or making love or worrying about the dentist. This is where my imagination balks." (*SC*, 216)

For Styron it is where all imaginations should balk. Stingo reflects back on the day Sophie arrived at Auschwitz, April 1, 1943, asks himself what he was doing that day, and realizes he was gorging himself on bananas trying to make himself heavy enough for the Marines. The subtle humor of skinny Stingo's "plight," wherein he incurs a snotty remark from an old recruiting sergeant, forms an ironic contrast to the horror of Sophie, though we do not know it at this point in the novel, selecting which of her children is to be exterminated at virtually the same moment. Immediately thereafter he shifts to another date—October 3, 1943. On that date he was writing a letter to his father concerning the fact that the Rose Bowl game might again be played at Duke University. For Sophie, it is the anniversary of the date of her marriage to Casmir Zawistowski. But, for 2,100 Greek Jews at Auschwitz-Birkenau it is the day of their incineration. Such thinking as this is Transfer in its most fundamental form, the reverse pivot on what Arendt suggested Nazi officials and soldiers were doing. Instead of saying what horrors I have been put through in pursuance of my duties (and so removing guilt by shifting the object of pain and suffering) rather ask "what would it be like if I, and not they, were the ones enduring the pain and suffering I am dispensing or is being dispensed by someone else?" This, Styron would say is Transfer, inserting oneself in the place of those at whose expense one's own personal Fortune quest is able to be pursued.

Such transference unites man with his brother and reduces his position as what I have called "The Solitary"; it reminds him of the shifting nature of Fortune; it suggests that, however failed his own promises are in realizing themselves, they are better than those of his brothers; he understands that Fortune-forcing can only make his brother's condition yet worse; he feels guilt; in feeling guilt he ceases the evil he is producing and, perhaps, begins to rediscover God; he has no reason to lie. Stated simply, Transfer is man's ability to imagine himself in the position of the recipient of the evil his own lack of guilt enables him to produce, tolerate, or ignore.

Just as Sophie called her father the source of all evil, Stingo's father seems to be the antithetical symbol of good, of Transfer. Where his own personal politics, for example, suggest that he should castigate and disassociate himself from the right-wing racist Frank Hobbs, he still sees him first of all as a human being. Though his politics are "ten miles to the right of Mussolini" (*SC*, 107), Hobbs, for Stingo's father, is still a " 'good ole boy,' [yet] . . . a tragic man, lonely, a widower, and still mourning the death of his only child. . . . " (*SC*, 107–8) Hobbs, in return, can equally transcend the apparent division between them and will his friendly adversary his peanut farm. And Stingo's father, having no need for such nor for the money it might fetch at auction, offers it to Stingo, whom he knows, though over twenty-one, is not financially ready to be so. Contrary to Sophie's father, who sees her as a typist and pamphlet hawker, Stingo's father maintains steady contact with his son, despite his choice to live in the North, and midway through the novel yields to his own need "to re-establish, face to face, eyeball to eyeball, our mutual love and kinship." (*SC*, 188)

On his trip to New York the old gentleman instructs his son in several matters after he manages to get into an altercation with an insensitive cabbie. In each episode, Styron again reveals his highly-developed ability to Transfer. He reminds Stingo, for instance, that the North is just as prejudiced as the South is—a typical piece of Southern defensiveness, one might say—except that Stingo is quick to say as well that his father "had never been given to shifting unreasonably the various racial evils of the South onto the shoulders of the North," that he was a "lifelong Southern liberal." (*SC*, 289) In 1947 this last phrase would have been a contradiction in terms for most people, but not for Stingo's father. It is a prime example of his ability to Transfer, to escape the approach to life which would be most comfortable for him (and perhaps most uncomfortable for many others) and view human existence from the other side. Contrast this to Arendt's statements about the Nazi functionaries who could actually shift the sympathy for Jewish pain onto themselves.

What of the confrontation with the cabbie? Again I think, however ludicrous the event ultimately became, the right rests with Stingo's father. When the cabbie calls him a "fucking asshole" for a nickel tip, the older man's sense of man's duty to his fellow man has been shaken. He is appalled by the attitude and reacts against it, quite unlike those in, say, Poland at the time of Auschwitz who, if not incarcerated, can understand the camp as an asset to the local economy or, if an inmate, can slog through the shifting sands of Fortune in search of a foothold for themselves alone. " 'Detestable scum that you are, you are no more civilized than a sewer rat! In any decent place in the United States a person like you disgorging your disgusting filth would be taken out in a public square and horsewhipped!' " (*SC*, 293) If such a statement at first seems simply divisive, one need only reflect that it is a reminder to the cabbie of his own self-lowered place on the Chain of Being, as well as a reminder that other human beings have rights and dignity and perhaps need for a nickel as well. It is a demand, in short, that both the cabbie and the passenger be accorded an equal place on the human scale. It is the instructive dimension of Transfer.

Nor is it the only scene in which we see the elder man provide such instruction. Consider the episode when, to have a ride in a friend's convertible, Stingo forgot to stoke the fire for his sickly mother, only to return later to find her suffering from a severe chill. Stingo's punishment? "The blood-congealing cold and darkness of the woodshed where he marched me and where he made me stay until long after darkness fell over the village and frigid moonlight seeped in through the cracks of my cell. . . . I was only aware that I was suffering exactly in the same way that my mother had and that my deserts could scarcely be more fitting. . . . " (*SC*, 297) This is Transfer.

Generally, however, Styron does not seem to suggest that Transfer is something which must be learned. It seems rather a natural human instinct which the solitary pursuit of Fortune has repressed in men and nations. Emmi Höss suddenly responds to Sophie, after she collapses, as a human rather than as a "Polack." Larry Landau worries about his brother's dementia rather than see him as a disgrace to a respectable and otherwise Fortune-blessed family. Blackstone sees to virtually every need Sophie has before she meets Nathan, and she supports him emotionally—at severe cost to herself—when his wife is killed. Nathan freely gives Stingo money as a gift when his band-aid box bank is pilfered. Even Morris Fink, full of ethnic slurs and tales out of school, can respond with human determination when he smells the final trouble developing with Sophie and Nathan. And, on the novel's final page, a group of otherwise rowdy young boys has taken the trouble to cover the drunken Stingo with sand to keep him warm until he awakens on Coney Island Beach. They could have picked his pocket.

Several characters stand out as people who, like Stingo's father, live by the principle of Transfer continuously rather than occasionally. Yetta Zimmerman imposes as few rules as possible upon her tenants—"'What I like to see is my tenants enjoy life'" (*SC*, 34)—but she demands that her own humanity be respected as well—"'You be a gentleman and quiet and have [the girl in your room] out of there at a reasonable hour, you'll have no quarrel with Yetta about a girl in your room.'" (*SC*, 34) Never in thirty years has she evicted anybody, except of course the "weird *oysvorf*" she caught in 1938 "'dressed up in girls' panties.'" (*SC*, 161) Another such person is Wanda who tries relentlessly to break down the barriers which prevent human beings from such Transfer. As Sophie realizes in retrospect, Wanda and her brother, Jozef, were "two selfless, courageous people whose allegiance to humanity and their fellow Poles and concern for the hunted Jews were a repudiation of all that her father had stood for." (*SC*, 372) Nor will Wanda turn on Sophie despite her refusal to aid in the cause of resistance and despite the death of Jozef while fighting for it. She can still be tender and consoling when Sophie, at Auschwitz, is desperate over Jan's welfare.

Perhaps all the themes I have been discussing come to a head in the character Stingo names Dr. Fritz Jemand Von Niemand, who provides Sophie with her titular "Choice." Alone on the platform at Auschwitz, he is Fortune's darling. He is rich, he is a doctor, he decides who shall live and who shall die, he controls Fortune. Thousands of other people are at his mercy. He is free of guilt and seems to have no reason to curse God nor to lie about his failures. He is as close to playing the role of God as an earthly man can get. But he is drunk, and his soul is ravaged. He is so isolated at the top that he is no longer a human. He cannot feel the guilt which will allow him to re-establish contact with his fellow man and with the real God if there is one. If Stingo's interpretation is the correct one—and surely in thematic terms it must be—in giving Sophie her choice he is simply trying to commit the greatest atrocity against mankind that he can think of, against one suffering being instead of against the faceless masses whom he turns into smoke, and thereby experience guilt for the first time in many monotonous years and so become human again.

In the final analysis, however, Von Niemand is seeking what young Stingo himself searches for throughout *Sophie's Choice*: the ability to turn himself away from the lonely quest for Fortune's rewards and toward a brotherhood with his fellow man in a racial endurance against the atrocities Fortune offers instead. Perhaps, without human assistance—without inhuman cabbies and librarians, without each man trying to better himself at the cost of another, without Southern bigotry and Polish anti-Semitism and the Nazi Holocaust—perhaps Fortune might reveal herself to deal more favorably and more equitably than the history of the world has yet allowed man to believe she has or can or will.

Notes

1. *Sophie's Choice* (New York: Random House, 1979). All page references are to this edition. An objection to this novel has frequently been that it is disunified in subject and theme. For example, John W. Aldridge, reviewing for *Harper's*, remarks about such matters as the Leslie Lapidus episodes by saying "while there is a certain dismal comedy in all this, just what it has to do with the central story of Sophie is never made clear, evidently because Styron does not know." ("Styron's Heavy Freight," *Harper's*, Sept., 1979, p. 97) I am attempting here to respond to such criticisms as well as interpret the various dimensions of the novel's themes.

2. William Faulkner, *Absalom, Absalom!* (New York: The Modern Library, 1936), p. 127.

3. Cf., for example, Pearl K. Bell, "Evil & William Styron," *Commentary*, August, 1979, pp.57–59. "Each of [Styron's] novels was charged with an apocalyptic sense of evil, and this may perhaps explain Styron's fascination with the most diabolical events of the century." Also, Lazar Ziff, "Breaking Sacred Silences," *Commonweal*, 11 May 1979, pp. 277–78. "*Sophie's Choice,* then, continues on from *Nat Turner*; it is a further study of the intrusion into human history of an evil so enormous that historical determination alone is inadequate to account for it."

2

"HUMAN DIGNITY" AS THE ROOT OF ALL EVIL
A Reinterpretation of *The Confessions of Nat Turner*

Before examining the realization of Styron's major themes in the work which immediately preceded *Sophie's Choice,* I would like to fix more firmly what the concept of Transfer is and is not, and why Steiner's term "time-relation" is not conterminous with it.

Transfer is *not* simple Christian charity as it might at first appear, although that admired virtue might be an occasional by-product of it. Rather, Transfer is Styron's answer to the sort of difficulty Freud addresses in Chapter 5 of *Civilization and Its Discontents.* Adopting a "naive attitude" toward the concept of Christian charity, Freud writes:

> "Thou shalt love thy neighbor as thyself." . . . We find ourselves unable to suppress a feeling of astonishment, as at something un-natural. Why should we do this? What good is it to us? Above all, how can we do such a thing? How could it possibly be done? My love seems to me a valuable thing which I have no right to throw away without reflection. It imposes obligations on me that I must be prepared to make sacrifices to fulfill. If I love someone he must be worthy of it in some way or other. . . . But if he is a stranger to me and cannot attract me by any value he has in himself or any significance he may already have acquired in my emotional life, it will be hard for me to love him.[1]

Freud, in short, finds no rationality in this instruction of Christ, which has been "promulgated with such solemnity." It is not natural to mankind; and, even if it were, love so diluted and thinly spread would, for any given recipient, produce "only a small modicum of love [which would] fall to his lot."

For Freud, a different understanding is needed, so he offers to word the injunction of Christ differently: "If the high sounding ordinance had run: Love thy neighbor as thy neighbor loves thee, I should not take objection to it." This would at least relieve what Freud calls the *"Credo, quia absurdum"* aspect of Christianity, namely the corollary which amounts to "Just because thy neighbor is not worthy of thy love, is probably full of enmity towards thee, thou shouldst love him as thyself."[2] Nothing, says Freud, is more completely against the fundamental human nature than this.

In yielding this position, Styron in his fiction is seeking an alternative, for even Freud's "I will love my neighbor to the degree he loves me" is an invitation to conflict and retribution. Freud understands man to be naturally aggressive, and as such civilization denies him release for a basic drive. Hence, man is "discontent" within civilization:

> If civilization requires such sacrifices, not only of sexuality but also of the aggressive tendencies in mankind, we can better understand why it should be so hard for men to feel happy in it. In actual fact, primitive man was better off in this respect, for he knew nothing of any restrictions on his instincts. As a set-off against this, his prospects of enjoying his happiness for any length of time were very slight. Civilized man has exchanged some part of his chances for happiness for a measure of security.[3]

Furthermore, for both Styron and Freud, the reason why this sacrifice of happiness for security has not worked as well as it might is simply due to another way in which civilization has coped ineffectually with fundamental human nature. To quote Freud one last time, "in the primal family only the head of it enjoyed . . . instinctual freedom; the other members lived in slavish thraldom."[4] Civilization may have greatly corrected this imbalance in everyday social intercourse, but it cannot alter human nature. Because of this, we get, both in life and (consequently) in Styron's fiction, individual human beings insisting that the sacrifice of happiness and freedom for security be done by others, the "many" who are destined to live in "slavish thraldom." For the Solitary, the "head" instinct takes over, and he or she is then drawn into the major agonies of human existence that Styron investigates. To paraphrase numerous critics, I suggest that one of these is the desire to enslave other men which in Styron ranges from Helen Loftis' need to subjugate her daughter and her husband, to Mason Flagg's reduction of Cass Kinsolving to groveling fool, to the white race enslaving the black one, to the Master Race exterminating the Chosen People. Such thinking, such behavior, such terminology all underscore the horror of what human existence could become, first, if primal nature were allowed to exert itself and, second, if an acceptable substitute for the unrealistic Christian dictum (or "golden rule") were not found and practiced.

Transfer, then, does not ask that any man *love* his neighbor, though that could result; rather it asks only that he trade places with him in his imagination, that he empathize with him. Perhaps the Christian equivalent is "There but for the grace of God go I." Still, there is a dimension of relief and a feeling of luckiness that is embedded in the way that line is usually spoken, and these would not be constructive to Transfer. In a sense, then, Transfer, to the degree that it produces a climate for mutual respect and protection, is not entirely unselfish in its motives; but its results happily appear that way.

"Time-relation," then, is fully embraced by the concept of Transfer, but it is narrower. It asks only that one alert his or her mind to the existence of misery and evil at the very moment one might be inclined to create, tolerate, or ignore still more of it. Transfer asks that one's imagination and understanding escape the boundaries of time and place to "experience" that evil and misery in order that that ability to create evil might progressively be squeezed into the remotest corners of the human heart and soul. If Freud is correct, it can never be forced entirely out.

I would like to turn now to *The Confessions of Nat Turner* to demonstrate how Styron is only secondarily examining the struggles of a black slave to gain his rightful place in the human race. Primarily, based on the instructions we have been given in *Sophie's Choice,* his focus would rather seem to be on the struggle of a *human being,* his color entirely beside the point, to escape "the slavish thraldom" of most people into the condition of "primal head," the person who is entitled to "instinctual freedom" where others are not. Nat is seeking the realization of promises that all of Styron's Solitaries are. My basic contention will be that Styron recognized this in the historical Nat as well and so created his fictional one as he did.

The Historical Nat

One of the most fundamental mistakes that many critics had been making, I think, in their reading of *The Confessions of Nat Turner* is that Styron's "meditation on history" was meant to emphasize history *as fact*. Hence, William E. Akin is typical in his objection to Styron's sense of history when he states that "it is of primary importance that Turner be seen in his uniqueness, as an individual, not as an archetype making archetypal response to a universal situation."[5] Equally off the mark, I think, is C. Hugh Holman's criticism of the narrative point of view in the novel: "Styron's decision to operate from a single and interior point of view flaws the novel artistically because it blurs the social reality within which the Southampton insurrection occurred."[6] I think, then, that too much has been made of Nat Turner as a Negro slave *qua* Negro slave. Nat Turner is a man, a human being. So is Sophie. So is Hitler, however much we do not, as men ourselves, like to own up to that fact. Each, as most humans do, perceives the world about him or her as being amiss. Now surely Nat, who lives in bondage, and Sophie, a victim of an equivalent historical atrocity, have more right than most people do to feel that things are indeed unjust. But Styron provides enough evidence in both novels to suggest that, even if Nat were a Richmond wheelwright and Sophie the concert pianist she wanted to become, they, simply because they are human, probably would not have been fulfilled. The stakes would simply have become higher. Akin errs when he fails to realize that Nat Turner is emblematic of mankind for Styron; and Holman, therefore, does as well when he insists that the reader should not have been confined to Nat's consciousness. On the contrary, however, Styron is suggesting we must get a feeling for Nat's own all-too-human sense of specialness, for few of us are as special to anyone else as we are to ourselves. Furthermore, it is the effect of this sense of specialness in certain people upon the course of history that Styron is most centrally "meditating" upon.

Although Styron read widely in researching his novel, Lawyer Thomas R. Gray's 1831 pamphlet, "The Confessions of Nat Turner," is clearly his most fundamental source, both in his own reading of it and in the readings of it given by other writers Styron knew of who had attempted to recount Nat's legend before him. A thoroughly-researched essay by Seymour L. Gross and Eileen Bender is very informative on this matter.[7] We need no reminding that Gray's pamphlet was community-serving and self-serving in the extreme; and to what degree Nat's actual confession, presuming that he made one, was "fully and voluntarily made"[8] must be questioned. Yet the portrait Gray gives of Turner through the chained slave's own words reveals the sense of specialness and solitariness that I am claiming is also the "ruling passion" of Styron's heroes.

One of the first things Nat supposedly "confesses" to Gray is a recount of an incident when, as a child, he fully outlined to some playmates an event which had taken place long before he was born. Upon overhearing this Nat's mother summons "others" to listen as well and all are "astonished." This "caused them to say in my hearing, I surely would be a prophet, as the Lord had shewn me things that had happened before my birth. And my father and mother strengthened me in this first impression, saying in my presence, *I was intended for some great purpose* . . ." [italics mine].[9] While to an extent we can attribute such as this to the hyper-religiosity of Nat's family, it does not exclude most human beings, for it is merely one way of phrasing the sense each individual has that he is somehow "god-ordained," even when he or she acknowledges no particular God to do the ordaining.

At least in the words Gray assigns to Nat, a number of other lines early in the confession verge on egomania. "Yet such was the confidence of the negroes in the neighborhood, even at this early period of my life, in my superior judgment, that they would often carry me with them when they were going on any roguery, to plan for them."[10] Nat, though, is ontologically above such things. "Having soon discovered to be great, I must appear so, and therefore studiously avoided mixing in society, and wrapped myself in mystery, devoting my time to fasting and prayer."[11] He eventually convinces himself that such as he are not placed on this earth as mere lagniappe, that he "was ordained for some great purpose *in the hands of the Almighty*" [italics mine].[12] When, after reciting the particulars of the debacle into which the insurrection degenerated, Gray asks him if he finds himself, now, to be mistaken. Nat's reply is: "Was not Christ crucified?"[13]

I fully realize that it will not be popular to take a martyr in the struggle for human liberty and suggest that he is, at bottom, fundamentally egocentric and self-serving. Styron's most characteristic theme, however, novel after novel, is that virtually all humans perceive themselves to be embroiled in a struggle for liberty—at its best the liberty to be who they perceive themselves to be or, at its worst, the liberty to impose who they are on others. This second sort of struggle, that of the oppressor to oppress, intensifies the need of the downtrodden—Negroes and Jews in Styron—to regain what fundamental liberties of color and creed they ought by cosmic design to possess. My argument would not be that Nat was wrong in rebelling but rather that freedom and equality for the black race was a sub-purpose, though one which, were it to eventuate, would "justify" his Solitary purposes just as Bilbo's highways "justified" his racism, Huey Long's hospitals "justified" his corruption, and Hitler's renewal of German nationalism "justified" the Holocaust.

Gray remarks near the end of his pamphlet that Nat, "for natural intelligence and quickness of apprehension, is surpassed by few men I have ever seen."[14] A generous line for a white bigot to assign to a black slave-felon. Near the end of his novel Styron draws a scene in which Gray gives Nat a Bible and actually shakes his hand. For many critics this is finally a recognition of Nat as a *man*. And that is Styron's point as well. Nat is not a Black—Nat is a man who happens to be black and not white or yellow. But the fact that we as readers have been reluctant to recognize is that, once Styron has accorded Nat the dignity of being a man, he must then recognize (and so must the reader) that Nat like all men will fall victim to what we might call "the pursuits of the Solitary" and actually *create* evil.

The Solitary Nat

One of the most respected studies of *The Confessions of Nat Turner* is Alan Holder's, though it ultimately claims that Styron's novel "despite its ambition fails as both history and literature."[15] I would contend, however, that Holder has grounded his study in the wrong questions because he did not have the guidance that *Sophie's Choice* provides. If my point about Nat (or anyone) as essentially solitary can be accepted, such statements as these by Holder become moot: "there is something disturbing in Styron's treatment of Nat and the Negro that one can feel without being a black militant. This is his portrayal of Nat's attitude toward his fellow slaves."[16] Holder goes on to inquire "how could Nat Turner who felt so alienated from his people have functioned as their leader, particularly in a dangerous enterprise?"[17] Holder was, I think, on the verge of answering his own question a page later, though he allowed it to evade him: "Nat's sensory impressions of the Negro often seem to be all that a white racist could ask for. . . . But, . . . there is little for the white racist to cheer about on the basis of such of its members as come within Nat's purview."[18] Holder is referring, of course, to Gray, Eppes, Ethelred T. Brantley, Nathaniel Francis, and others. Styron's point is rather, that they are all, black and white alike, simply "not-Nat."

This sense of self has been cultivated in Nat from his earliest days and is reinforced throughout his life. He separates himself from his playmates and even refuses to look at the line of Negroes going off to field work in the morning. Nat is a "house nigger" "contemptuous and aloof, filled with disdain for the black riffraff which dwells beyond the close perimeter of the big house." (*NT*, 136)[19] He has "soft pink palms" that never experience "the grimy feel of the hoe handle and the sickle and the ax." (*NT*, 167) He is "the little black jewel of Turner's Mill." (*NT*, 169) In a particularly meaningful scene he compares the Christmas gift *he* has received—a book—to those the other slaves are happily hauling in for themselves:

> Muffled up against the cold in the coarse and shapeless yet decent winter garments Marse Samuel provided for them, they straggled along in a single line, men, women, pickaninnies, prepared to receive

their gifts—a beanbag or a hunk of rock candy for the children, a yard of calico for the women, a plug of tobacco or a cheap jackknife for the men. . . . I could hear the babble of their voices, filled with Christmas anticipation, laughter high and heedless, and loutish nigger cheer. The sight of them suddenly touched me with a loathing so intense it was akin to disgust. . . . (*NT*, 174, italics Styron's)

While he does throw open his Bible now to a passage which commands him to *"ransom them from the power of the grave"* (*NT*, 174), there seems more a command in this to validate his own self image as something worthy of emulation and of superhuman power than to do humanitarian service for his suffering brother. In fact, much in the same way that Sophie feels relative security so long as there are Jews to die in her place at Auschwitz, so Nat is able to corner the better duties wherever he is (Eppes's farm excepted) because he has been taught wheel-making, carpentry, reading, and, in short, has been made—in his own words—"the smartest nigger in Southampton County." (*NT*, 343) In echo of Sophie he is "doubtless safe" (*NT*, 349) despite the fact that there are a half dozen slave traders snooping around the county.

So long as Nat is able to remain content with himself and his lot (at least by comparison with others), he feels in control of Fortune, its "darling" to quote Stingo. Yet as David Eggenschwiler pointed out in pursuit of another thesis entirely, Nat on occasion, even while quite young, senses his own true situation as human chattel, the brutishly hard life of the other Negroes despite his disdain for them as a group, and even a few hints of metaphysical injustice. "Nat repeatedly tries to replace that vision with neatly ordered and culturally conditioned stereotypes, to replace the terror of the irrational with melodramatic assurances of the known and simplified. But because these defenses are so contrived, they are often destroyed by a complex, minutely particularlized reality they can no longer contain."[20] Stated in the terms I established earlier, he begins to be aware that the promises he has made himself—and, in one key moment, that had been made *to* him by Sam Turner—are destined not to be realized.

When Nat says the following words with reference to Negro slaves, they pertain especially to them only insofar as they are more downtrodden than most other human beings; but in Styron's universe there is ultimately no color line here: "beat a nigger, starve him, leave him wallowing in his own shit, and he will be yours for life. Awe him by some unforeseen hint of philanthropy, tickle him with the idea of hope, and he will want to slice your throat." (*NT*, 70) The same is true of something Nat says later in the novel—again he attaches it to the word "Negro," but Styron would again suggest, via *Sophie's Choice*, that that word pertains only to signify a degree of awareness rather than a basic difference between the Negro and any other man: "I do not believe that I had ever thought of the future; it is not in the mood of a Negro, once aware of the irrecoverable fact of his bondage, to dwell on the future at all. . . . That something *different* might befall my lot had never occurred to me." (*NT*, 170–71, italics Styron's) For the Negro as for all men, the concept of "the Future," in other words of "promises" of change for the better, is what initiates the pattern of unrealizable expectations which causes men to set morality, reason, common sense, self-control, or other restraints upon the baser instincts aside.

Again I must insist that I am not arguing that Nat should have been a good darky and remained happy that he was cleaning up crumbs from a linen tablecloth rather than lugging cow manure from a field. Nor am I suggesting, in Styron's next work, that Sophie and those incarcerated at Auschwitz should simply have behaved themselves (as most did) and accepted their fate when it came. What I *am* suggesting is that once the promise of and consequent desire for something better is initiated, the Solitary reinforces his solitariness. With the possible exception of her son, Sophie has no plans whatsoever to bail out Wanda or Bronek or anyone else. She has never even told them about the anti-Semitic pamphlet that she believes can do the trick for her. Since Fortune's rewards are so few, the human instinct is not to divide them up any more than is necessary. The same is true of Nat Turner, not Negro slave, but human being—unfortunately not purged by his color of any of the human vices that make human existence the shambles it can become.

Consider the novel's central scene. Samuel Turner, trembling with emotion, makes Nat the greatest promise a black slave could have made to him: " 'I shall draw up the papers for your emancipation. You will then at age twenty-five be a free man. . . . I shall only stipulate that you return to Turner's Mill for a visit every blue moon or two—with whichever young darky girl you have taken for a wife!' " (*NT*, 193) Samuel Turner has *not* promised to free his slaves. He will free Nat. Nat can come back when he cares to shoot the breeze with those still in bondage. Nat is special to himself and to Turner and is willing to reap the benefits of that. No rebel here. In fact he immediately begins bragging about it all when they encounter a slave coffle which has halted along the side of the road on its way to Georgia. As some of the chained less-fortunate beg Nat for food, he tells one of them " 'My mastah's goin' to set me free in Richmond.' " After a bit of sarcastic banter, the man replies " 'Yo' shit stink too, sugah. Yo' ass black jes' like mine, honey chile.' " (*NT*, 200–1) Later, when Reverend Eppes fails to follow through in Samuel Turner's stead, Nat does not hate Eppes. Instead, "for Marse Samuel . . . the rage rose and rose in my breast until I earnestly wished him dead, and in my mind's eye I saw him strangled by my own hands." (*NT*, 246–47) Samuel Turner, after all, was the maker of the unrealized promised.

As he will eventually do in *Sophie's Choice,* Styron surrounds his characters with ever-present reminders of this promise/realization dichotomy in death-bound existence. Not only is Nat condemned to "nigger work" by Eppes, the Moores, and Travis, so is the land itself deteriorating. Because of haphazard tobacco farming, Virginia is "now utterly consumed by that terrible weed." (*NT*, 220) As a consequence the slaves who knew only the "better" life of Virginia are now transported south and separated from their families. In another example of Styron's insistence on this same theme we get the memorable section which deals with Hark's break for Pennsylvania, traveling for weeks (unwittingly in circles), avoiding towns, lying low, until he finally catches sight of what he believes to be the "Squash-honna" but is really "that ancient mother-river of slavery, the James." (*NT*, 286) And he is turned in by another Negro who, a human being also, is seeking gain for himself. Perhaps the most summarial example of the promise/realization theme is young Nat Turner spelling *Columbine* for an amazed white audience contrasted to his adult body strung from the gallows and later taken down for skinning to fashion a money purse for Mr. R. S. Barham's father.

If my employment of young Stingo's awarenesses in *Sophie's Choice* is a valid means by which to reinterpret *The Confessions of Nat Turner*, the regular next step in man's reaction to failed promises is Fortune-forcing, the attempt to get events back on track. In this novel, of course, the major example of that is Nat's rebellion itself. Here again I must take issue with the standard position that most critics have taken on the causes for this, of which Donald W. Markos' is an example: "Nat Turner's revolutionary intention was a long time in the brewing, his rebellion was a reaction to the emasculation of himself and his people."[21] I question whether "his people" were of central importance, or whether they were merely tools to aid him in a process—actualization of his own self-image—which could not be conducted alone, as a Solitary. Again the phrasing Nat uses is interesting. For example, as he stokes the hatred in the hearts of his four lieutenants, he says this of Hark:

> It was not easy to make of Hark a potential killer, to generate true hatred in that large-hearted breast. Without causing him, as I did, to brood on the sale of his wife and child, I might have failed. But of all the Negroes, Hark was the most surely and firmly under my domination. (*NT*, 334)

Note there is no reference to "we" failing—just "I." Note the phrase "my domination." Note the distress he purposely causes Hark. Nat, it would seem, is more important in his own mind than anyone else or the cause itself is. This is enlarged upon later when Will returns just in time to join the "ruction." According to Gray's document Will was a fully capable person who participated effectively for the duration of the rebellion. Styron's Nat sees him as deranged, however, and fears that he will lead the mission astray. He wishes him out of the way because "I could in no way control or govern him." (*NT*, 362) If the cause were primary, Nat would have admitted what is quickly evident once the killing begins—that Will *can* do it and so can gain the respect and leadership of the others and perhaps lead them effectively. Instead Nat fights for his own generalship; and, in response to Will's taunt that " 'less'n you kin make de *ax* sing a tune you is *all done*' " (*NT*, 408), he goes on to murder young Margaret Whitehead (the only person Nat *did* kill)to cement his power.

I am not claiming that in the long run Nat needs history to call this "Nat's Rebellion" and not Will's. Rather, Nat needs to assure himself that he *is* the Nat he thinks he is and has thought he was since his mother first showed him the difference between house niggers and field niggers and since Sam Turner first had him taught to spell and read. Nat will force events to take a very particular shape in order to protect that sacred self-image.

In the terms I employed in considering *Sophie's Choice*, the evil Nat now sets loose stems from his Solitary's inability to feel guilt; yet in contrast to the evildoers of the other novels—Mason Flagg, Colonel Templeton, Hitler, Von Niemand—Nat is virtually doomed to failure from the outset. He must be able to kill and do so liberally in order to effect his design, yet he cannot kill.

But why can Nat not kill? Is it that the very act of starting the ruction, which was something quite different when it was only a mental construct, has revealed to his hyper-developed sense of God what it is he is *really* about? Throughout his life he has seen a plethora of examples of "guiltlessness" from the general fact of white men owning black men to particularlized manifestations such as McBride's rape of his mother and Samuel Turner's selling off of his Negroes " 'out of the desperation to hang on pointlessly a few years longer.' " (*NT*, 221) He has even participated in a number of like actions himself, such as when he turned an inferior field slave away from Turner's front door and directed him "to the proper rear door in a voice edged with icy scorn." (*NT*, 169) Even as the other blacks around him were sold away from their families, he, like Sophie amidst hoards of exterminatable Jews, was able to keep up a "sunny optimism and complacency." (*NT*, 222) Now however, as he and his band stand over Travis and his wife in bed, Nat's ax poised to split their skulls, he, for the first time, has an entirely different reaction to his owner:

> Now I saw that beneath the perplexity, the film of sleep, his eyes were brown and rather melancholy, acquainted with hard toil, remote perhaps, somewhat inflexible but not at all unkind, *and I felt that I knew him at last*—maybe even now not well but far better than one knows another man by a pair of muddy trousers viewed from the level of the ground, or bare arms and hands, or a disembodied

voice. . . . I had a final glimpse of who he truly might be. Whatever else he was, *he was a man*. (*NT*, 387–88) [Italics mine]

Although Nat proceeds to utter the melodramatic line *"Thus art thou slain!"*, he brings the ax down awry and embeds it in the headboard between them. He had for the first time related to Travis *as a man*.

One of the most fundamental of all arguments against slave-holders is that they do not grant their human chattel full dignity *as men*. If they had admitted their humanity they could not have enslaved them in the first place. Akin has said that "the white slave-owner with the slightest sensitivity to mankind can only be re-deemed and freed from his guilt if the black man accepts his white owner's benevolent *noblesse oblige*."[22] This means I think that, for many slaveholders, there was a strong need to fight back the aware-ness of them as men by finally understanding them as only ap-proximations of men who simply could not take care of themselves and would rot in their freedom as Arnold and other freed Negroes are seen to do in this novel. But, once again, Styron seems to be asking the reader to remove the concept of skin color from this consideration and, in the scene above, realize that it is now black men in full control of the lives of a white couple. Brutalized by the system, Will, Hark, and others have had their humanity repressed and consequently underdeveloped; hence they can "make the axes sing," to use their words. They cannot see their victims *as men,* and hence they can readily create evil. Their victims are as killable as mosquitoes just as, for slaveholders, black men are as enslaveable as plowhorses. Yet in this scene we see Nat—better educated, more literate, more aware of God, permitted to become more human—unable to strike the blow with any accuracy. After repeated failures he later *does* kill Margaret Whitehead but with consummate inef-ficiency. He plunges a sword into her, missing the vitals entirely, and finally must club her to death with a fence rail to put her out of her misery. Shortly thereafter, as the carnage reaches a crescendo around him, Nat sees a "young girl of fourteen or so" run screaming out of the Harris farmhouse and turn toward the Williams farm to warn them. "I might have reached her in a twinkling . . . but I suddenly felt dispirited and overcome by fatigue, and was pursued by an obscure, unshakable grief. I shivered in the knowledge of the futility of all ambition. . . . Did I really wish to vouchsafe a life for the one that I had taken?" (*NT*, 417)

Later, in his cell, when Gray asks Nat whether he feels guilt for the loss of life his failed ruction has caused, Nat replies " 'I don't feel guilty'." (*NT*, 392) However, when left to his own thoughts, Nat is not so sure: "Is it true that I really have no remorse or contrition or guilt for anything I've done? Is it maybe because I have no remorse that I can't pray and that I know myself to be so removed from the sight of God?" (*NT*, 398)

I would like to draw two analogies with *Sophie's Choice* here to set a context for Styron's "solution" to the problem of human evil. First, on the matter of God and His existence, the two novels appear dissimilar; but actually, I think, they are not. Nat turns continually toward God and seeks His help and guidance. He finds omens in king snakes, eclipses, gunshots, clouds. When he is forced to change his plans for the day of the ruction, his initial disappointment and anger are quickly assuaged: "in His great wisdom He had caused me to wait for a grander day and the beginnings of an even more propitious design." (*NT*, 355) Yet once the ruction is underway and running out of control, Nat begins to question his God: "I had many times prayed to the Lord to spare me this fear, but now it was plain that, unheeding, He was going to allow me to suffer anyway this griping sickness, this clammy apprehension." (*NT*, 381–82) Later, in prison, he feels "as alone and as forsaken as I had ever felt since I had learned God's name." (*NT*, 402) In *Sophie's Choice* we recall that Sophie and Stingo spend much boozy time in the Maple Court saying much the same thing in harsher terminology, blaming God at bottom for miscreating the entire universe. "Fuck God" (*SC*, 500), Sophie finally writes in her letter of farewell to Stingo; and Stingo, more articulate on the matter, speaks of an "idiot's dream of God, or the idea that there could be such a Thing." (*SC*, 466)

On the most obvious level this is an oft-heard cry of despair over a God who would allow such things as human slavery or the Holocaust. It puts the blame solely on Him. On another level it seems to place man in God's place by implying that life should have taken the form that Stingo or Sophie or Nat Turner would more have approved of as a suitable "Divine Plan." But each book finally suggests that both levels are focusing on the wrong concerns and asking the wrong questions. Sophie, as we have seen, phrases the matter more appropriately for Styron when, about midway through the novel, she says " 'I don't know any more about *when* God leave me. Or I left Him'." (*SC*, 232) The issue is simply who left whom— Sophie in disgust with Him or He in disgust with her? Similarly Nat Turner says, in his final pages, "Maybe in this anguish of mine God is trying to tell me something. Maybe in His seeming absence He is asking me to consider something that I had not thought of or known before." (*NT*, 402)

The two works, then, would seem to arrive at the same position on God and, more importantly, on man's relation to Him. We can blame Him for ill-conceived creation or we can recognize that man in his solitary pursuit of Fortune's niggling handouts during his own lifetime has misshaped that plan as if he, the Solitary—in other words all men individually—were the designer of it and the teleological Good toward which it should be directed. Nat Turner and Sophie Zawistowska, then, simply fall victim to a world which has for centuries been similarly mishandled by Solitaries who have preceded them. Now, in human bondage in 1831 or a Nazi concentration camp in 1943, Nat and Sophie respond in kind, not for the good of their brothers or their race, but for the long climb up the pecking order that they have recognized in their given environments. Both Sophie, as a typist, and Nat, as "the smartest nigger in Southampton County," are literally "house slaves." They are "better" and plan to gain by that. Hitler was Aryan, Bilbo white, Sophie's father influential, McBride in authority, Travis the fortunate beneficiary of another man's untimely death: all humans have their own springboards upward. And being human, they will all use them, be they white, black, Jewish, Catholic, Baptist, Rebel or Yankee.

Once again the fundamental step out of one's solitary, egocentric, evil-doing universe is the concept of Transfer I discussed earlier. It asks the Solitary to evaluate the world from other perspectives than his own purview. It asks that he be aware of the suffering of others by mutually sharing it, that he do something about it if he can, that he cease causing it if he is about the business of "Fortune-forcing" at the expense of others. If in *Sophie's Choice* it transfers Stingo into the bodies and minds of those aspiring writers whose manuscripts he is decimating, in the present novel it asks that Nat Turner recognize the full responsibilities of the human equality he rightly demands. And, of course, it demands that the slaveholder imagine falling to his knees in a pool of pig slop while his back takes the lash of the bullwhip. Until they and all men are capable of Transfer, human evil will overpower human goodness.[23]

In *The Confessions of Nat Turner,* several characters approach Transfer. Judge Cobb leaves badly shaken after hearing of and viewing Hark's special plight, and Nat resolves not to kill him as a result. Samuel Turner understands what bondage must be for Nat who is at least as intelligent as he is and, so, vows to set him free. Margaret Whitehead, to the extent that she understands and believes the moralisms of her chatter, transfers. Perhaps even Lawyer Gray is on the verge of it when, as his last gesture, he brings Nat a Bible and shakes his hand.

But it is Nat with whom the reader identifies, and the epiphany of Transfer must ultimately be his. We have seen earlier that he has recognized Travis' humanity for the first time as he stands with an ax poised above him—and so Nat misses when he swings. Earlier he has befriended Willis in hopes of raising him to a higher level as well. "It would be hard to describe how much it pleased me to think of Willis free like myself in the city, the two of us dedicated to spreading God's word among the black people and to honest work in the employ of the white." (*NT,* 207) He has baptized Ethelred T. Brantley, whom no white preacher will go near, and even warns him to stay clear when the ruction eventually materializes. He has put a crushed turtle out of its misery. Yet the most significant, and the final, experience of Transfer is his recollection of Margaret Whitehead on the day of his execution.

At the moment he killed her he had seen in her gaze "a grave and drowsy tenderness such as I had never known, [she] spoke some words too soft to hear and, saying no more, closed her eyes upon all madness, illusion, error, dream, and strife." (*NT,* 415) After he flung away the rail with which he clubbed her to death, he continued to circumnavigate the field in which her body lay and thought he "saw her rise from the blazing field with arms outstretched" crying " 'Oh, I would fain swoon into an eternity of love!' " (*NT,* 415) Now, as he awaits the hangman, Nat lies in his cell and has one last masturbatory fantasy about Margaret which critics, black and white alike, have too facilely dismissed as a white Southern bigot's rendition of what "really" goes on in the mind of a young black buck who lusts after the bodies of pure white women. Rather, I think, it is Transfer: "I tremble and I search for her face in my mind, seek her young body, yearning for her suddenly with a rage that racks me with a craving beyond pain; with tender stroking motions I pour out my love within her; pulsing flood; she arches against me, cries out, *and the twain—black and white—are one.*" (*NT,* 426) [Italics mine] As he approaches the gallows he feels her entreating him to heaven where they will love one another eternally. His last thoughts are confused, as he tries to reassure himself what he has done was right despite it all. But the presence of Margaret still dominates his vision, and his final thoughts of her are stated in religious terms. *"I would have destroyed them all. Yet I would have spared one. I would have spared her that showed me Him whose presence I had not fathomed or maybe never even known. Great God, how early it is! Until now I had almost forgotten His name."* (*NT,* 428, italics Styron's)

The purpose of this analysis has not been to de-emphasize the atrocity of Negro slavery nor to diminish the role played by the real Nat Turner in demanding that that atrocity be recognized and dealt with. Nor is it an attempt to confront directly the black (and white) critics who have charged Styron with racism (though I think they are totally incorrect).[24] Rather its purpose has been to argue that, in insisting on Nat's stature and dignity as a human being— that which has been denied anyone who is in bondage to another man—Styron's primary purpose was to show Nat enveloped by the misunderstandings that almost all men and women have been historically enveloped by in their attempts to gain what they perceive to be their just deserts. It was not until *Sophie's Choice,* however, that Styron made fully clear to his readers, and perhaps to himself, exactly what has been going wrong all along.

Negro slavery and the Holocaust are simply extreme manifestations of an ongoing historical pattern—the need of all humans to
enslave other humans so that their own solitary expectations may
be met in the face of Fortune's careless disregard of them. In the
sense that most people do not deem their expectations (promises)
properly realized, they consider themselves historical victims, even
if not black or Jewish. As a result they begin "forcing Fortune" and
in the process weaken their sense of guilt. The result is Evil and
ever greater separation from God or whatever their personal standard of Right and Goodness is. To assure themselves that they are
correct in what they are about, they invent constructs which lend
cosmic significance to what is really personal gratification or, at
least, the quest of it. They heighten their solitariness and, by cor-
relation, their division from other men. The lives of other men, to
quote again from Stingo's research, come to be seen in the light of
"absolute expendability." (*SC*, 235)

What Nat comes close to understanding and what Stingo does
finally realize is that there is only one way to reverse the process.
Call it time-relation or Transfer or whatever you will, it is simply
the active attempt to escape the confines of one's own Solitary vision
and to see and know and experience the pain in the worlds of others
which is equivalent to one's own and, perhaps, much more than
equivalent. As Nat cries out to his jailers as they take the crippled
Hark to the gallows, "'You've done hurt him enough! All his life!
Now God damn you don't hurt him no more!'" (*NT*, 427)

Notes

1. Sigmund Freud, *Civilization and Its Discontents*, trans. Joan Riviere, *Great
Books of the Western World*, ed. Mortimer Adler (Chicago: Encyclopaedia Britan-
nica, Inc., 1952), LIV, 786.
2. Freud, p. 786.
3. Freud, p. 788.
4. Freud, p. 788.

5. William E. Akin, "Toward an Impressionistic History: Pitfalls and Possibilities in William Styron's Meditation on History," *American Quarterly,* 21 (1969), 807–8.

6. C. Hugh Holman, *The Immoderate Past: The Southern Writer and History* (Athens: University of Georgia Press, 1977), p. 89.

7. Seymour L. Gross & Eileen Bender, "History, Politics, and Literature: The Myth of Nat Turner," in *The Achievement of William Styron,* eds. Robert K. Morris and Irving Malin (Athens: University of Georgia Press, 1975), pp. 168–207.

8. Thomas R. Gray, "The Confessions of Nat Turner," as reprinted in *William Styron's Nat Turner: Ten Black Writers Respond,* ed. John Henrik Clarke (Boston: Beacon Press, 1968), from the reproduced title page. Gray's document covers pp. 90–117 of this volume.

9. Gray, p. 99.

10. Gray, p. 101.

11. Gray, p. 101.

12. Gray, p. 101.

13. Gray, p. 104.

14. Gray, p. 113.

15. Alan Holder, "Styron's Slave: *The Confessions of Nat Turner,*" *South Atlantic Quarterly,* 68 (1969), 167–80.

16. Holder, p. 171.

17. Holder, p. 172.

18. Holder, p. 173.

19. *The Confessions of Nat Turner* (New York: Random House, 1967). All page numbers refer to this edition.

20. David Eggenschwiler, "Tragedy and Melodrama in *The Confessions of Nat Turner,*" *Twentieth-Century Literature,* 20 (1972), 20.

21. Donald W. Markos, "Margaret Whitehead in *The Confessions of Nat Turner,*" *Studies in the Novel,* 4 (1972), 57.

22. Akin, pp. 808–9.

23. Styron's most thoroughgoing exploration of this dualism in man is in *Set This House on Fire.*

24. See especially Clarke, et al., n. 8.

3

FORCED MARCHES

"Marriott, the Marine" and *The Long March*

After the publication of *The Confessions of Nat Turner* in 1967, Styron's next novel was to have been something entitled *The Way of the Warrior*. He, in fact, published just under twenty thousand words of it in the September, 1971, *Esquire* under the title of "Marriott, the Marine," subheaded "*Semper Fi! A* selection from the forthcoming novel *The Way of the Warrior*."[1] Opposite the first page of the story is a full-page black-and-white photograph of a butch-cut, sinister-eyed, heavily-decorated Marine lieutenant colonel primly holding a demitasse cup and saucer with pinky and ring finger affectedly extended. The sidelong glance, however, suggests beachheads, landings, random carnage. The picture's ambiguity hints at the promise-realization theme I have been exploring; but, more importantly, so does the story—in spades. Although the novel, to this date, has yet to appear, it would seem that Styron's themes, delineated most clearly in *Sophie's Choice*, will develop along a consistent course.

In a 1974 interview with Ben Forkner and Gilbert Schricke,[2] Styron mentioned that at that point he had already set *The Way of the Warrior* aside. In answer to the question "what did you start working on next?" after *Nat Turner*, Styron replied:

> Well, I officially began writing a novel having to do with the Marine Corps and I'd written a great number of pages, but somewhere along the line I'd gotten totally sidetracked curiously because I suddenly realized that what I was doing wasn't motivating me

deeply enough. So I had to interrupt this work to do something that I'm doing which is the work I told you about, the book about Poland.[3]

In answer to the ensuing question as to whether the new work would be a tragedy as his three major novels had been, Styron said of *Sophie's Choice*: "Well, the new book starts off very light in tone, not light but with a sort of ironic humor involved in it. But it touches on very tragic scenes and in a curious way is an extension of *Nat Turner*."[4]

Styron may have abandoned the Marine Corps story at that time, but he did not abandon his overriding subject, his central themes, his literary form, or the use of ironic humor to preface what would seem to be the impending darkness of his plot. In fact, the similarities of the first twenty-thousand words of the first version of *The Way of the Warrior* and roughly that many of *Sophie's Choice* are striking.

"Marriott, the Marine" is told by an unnamed narrator, though once again it is clearly Styron and, to the extent that Styron is Stingo, Stingo also. Instead of using himself as a new arrival in New York in 1947, however, he shifts the date to 1951, the year in which both Styron and the narrator were called back into Marine retraining for the Korean War. By this point the narrator has already completed and is reading proof on the novel Stingo was writing throughout *Sophie's Choice*: at one point he reads the reviews of, as one early bird has put it, "This fat, confident, deafening novel by a young Virginian." It has "received such florid advance raves that it is bound to be widely discussed and widely read even though its author's talent—while by no means inconsiderable—hardly measures up to the extravagant claims being made for it." (MM, 207)[5] The reviewer accuses it of having a "glacial pace" and places it among the "doom-despair-decay school of Southern letters." Though devastated by this mixed reception, the narrator, like Stingo, has already in the story confided to others that he "feared that my work still betrayed rhythms and echoes of my predecessors—mainly Faulkner and Fitzgerald" (MM, 200), and these rhythms lead the same reviewer to call him "hardly the literary original." (MM, 207) If there is any doubt left that this narrator is the same almost-Styron that

Stingo is, the story's opening paragraph is virtually unchallengeable. "A number of years ago I wrote a fictional narrative based loosely on this period in my life [the Marine recall and its rendition in *The Long March*], and it is possible that those who may have read that work will, in the account that follows, discern a few familiar echoes since I am certain to trespass here and there upon that earlier, restless mood." (MM, 101) Also reminiscent of the opening chapters of *Sophie's Choice* is the narrator's tirade against book reviewers, each of whom he describes in terms that could just as easily fit the manuscript-mutilating Stingo of the novel Styron turned to write instead: one he accuses of "looking down her snoot at every American novelist since Melville." (MM, 207)

The reason I pursue these analogies is to suggest that the excerpt entitled "Marriott, the Marine" and the novel that will apparently be completed and be Styron's next offering are products of the same time and thinking as *Sophie's Choice*, which I have placed as the keystone of this study.

The story as it has so far been published amounts to this: the narrator has just received orders to report to Camp Lejeune, North Carolina, for upgrading and eventual shipment to Korea. As in *The Long March*, the hero is distraught—not because he is well-entrenched in the business world and married (neither of which he is)—but because he is on the verge of seeing publication of his first novel and is about to become the "toast of the world, flattered, fussed over, with a thick wallet and suavely tailored flannels, dining at the Colony and Chambord and plowing my way through galaxies of movie starlets and seraglios of wenchy Park Avenue matrons perishing with need of my favors." (MM, 102) Instead, clad in an ill-fitting, moth-eaten uniform, he gets himself roundly drunk in a New York bar while MacArthur's welcome-home parade thunders by outside. The narrator's own impending fear contrasts sharply to the glorious survival of the fired (though returned) MacArthur:

. . . in an open Cadillac, flanked by shoals of motorcycle outriders, the ornate headpiece half an inch atilt as he saluted the mob with his corncob pipe, he fleetingly grimaced, gazing straight at me, and behind the raspberry-tinted sunglasses his eyes appeared as glassily opaque and mysterious as those of an old, sated lion, pensively digesting a wildebeest or, more exactly, like those of a man whose thoughts had turned inward upon some Caesarean dream magnified beyond compare. (MM, 102)

When the narrator arrives at camp, he immediately takes up, as Captain Mannix does, with others of his own ilk, officers who are reluctant and angry at having to participate in a situation in which "for the second time in less than a decade we were faced with the prospect of an ugly death." (MM, 104) In a short time, however, he is buttressed by two new friends: first, an equal named Lacy Dunlop who survives by knowing that others of his kind have it worse, for one reason or another, than he does; and, second, by a career officer named Lieutenant Colonel Paul Marriott who, though he has participated in virtually every famous operation that the Marines had been involved in in the previous fifteen years, has also read Faulkner, Flaubert, literary criticism about them, and speaks French impeccably. Marriott reads the proofsheets of the narrator's novel and praises it in informed terms. As the narrator is ruefully forced to admit, "maybe I was always too quick to sell the Marine Corps short." (MM, 200)

Marriott's image is even enough to offset the more "typical" Marine with whom the narrator is eventually forced to bunk: Second Lieutenant Darling P. Jeeter, Jr., USMC. A loutish individual who has joined up to do some legalized knife-fighting against "gooks," Jeeter has the polish of a discarded reaper blade. He even moves his terminally-ill father into their small quarters to cough himself into a bloody demise while the narrator tends to him in Jeeter's absence.

The resolution and epiphany in this much of *The Way of the Warrior* comes in a conversation the hero has with Marriott in which he rues his inability to help the elder Jeeter. When Marriott discovers who the man was—Stud Jeeter, Gunner Jeeter, he went by many names it turns out—he falls into awed remembrance of him, despite the fact that, in his day, the old fellow had made the world unsafe for every vital organ and tissue from human hearts and intestines to multinational maidenheads. As the highly-literate Marriott launches into an encomium on this " 'boozer, brawler, whoremonger . . . [who was] one of the best men with a heavy-machine-gun unit the Corps ever produced' "(MM, 210), the narrator suddenly sees him as "one of those pukka sahib types . . . memorializing vanished exploits on the Afghan border." (MM, 210) Crushed with disappointment at the true colors of his new-found idol, the hero comes to realize "how foolish it was for me to feel that way: he was a marine above all, first and foremost, *always* a marine, and for me it had been the dreamiest wishful thinking, goofy as a schoolgirl's, to see him as truly 'literary' or 'artistic' when these were merely components of an enlightened and superior dilettantism." (MM, 210) Though at the end he continues to admire Marriott for not having the finer graces entirely crushed out of him by the "all-molding pressures of the military system" (MM, 210), he further understands that "Paul was certainly at least as comfortable, if not more so, when talking of these matters [killing and whoremongering] as about French cuisine or the gentle art of fiction." (MM, 210) And here the story, as we presently have it, ends.

It is in this final contradiction, or dichotomy, or irony—call it what you will—that Styron returns to one of his most central and unifying themes: the stark contrast between the good and beauty mankind is capable of in its finest moments and the real filth and ugliness it can degenerate to at others, from seminary-student/ex-terminators like Von Niemand, to preacher/murderers like Nat Turner, to artist/drunkards like Cass Kinsolving. And, much like Styron's other work, it seems to be both the course of history and historical example which suppress that finer side at the critical moments of individual and racial development. As the narrator of this story says, "it seemed to me that all of us were both exemplars and victims of some uncontrollable aggression, a hungry will for bloodshed creeping not only throughout America but the world, and I could not help but abruptly shiver in that knowledge." (MM, 104)

The hero of this story is a slightly different sort of Solitary from most of Styron's other central characters. His predecessors and even his lone successor, Stingo, all convey the attitude of expectation that, now that they have attained the age of adulthood, the childhood forecasts for them, self-made or otherwise, will begin to come true. The hero here, however, sees himself as a man who has been expected to pay unforeseen dues for his happiness (participation in World War II), has paid in full, and as a consequence has begun to collect as promised in his bound-to-be-successful first novel. The wheel of Fortune, in other words, *has* circled to the top; but now it is proceeding inevitably toward its nadir, much sooner than the hero could have predicted (if he had anticipated that at all). In fact, he feels himself trapped between two worlds in his present situation, one of which he yearns for and the other which he detests, but both of which are heavily populated by people totally happy to be in them. I speak of the world he has left, the pleasures of Park Avenue fame and the satisfactions of the beach on Fire Island with his girlfriend Laurel, and the world of the military, the rugged, amoral, comradely microcosm of the professional warrior. At Camp Lejeune, of course, the world he prefers is much less proximate than the one he does not. He seeks out those who are in a similar frame of mine, Lacy Dunlop most centrally, and lingers with them or mopes alone in his room, in "despair over new rumors that we were soon to ship out for Korea and by a general sense of doom and frustration that had begun to overtake me more often as the summer passed. . . ."(MM, 204) He feels a sharp contrast to the lives of the local "fortune's darlings," the regular officers whose homes are near-by, whose wives are in bed with them, and whose outlook is sufficiently narrow to make latent carnage a tolerably-profitable way of life.

Two characters cause him to question, though only momentarily, his self-pitying estimation of his own existence. Lacy Dunlop has his "Misery List" on which he attempts to rank objectively the true degree of failed promise in each of his reluctant-warrior comrades' lives. He finds neither the narrator nor himself very high on it. The narrator has gotten his book written and hence has a "hope for some small immortality" (MM, 104), has some money, is an officer instead of an enlisted man. Dunlop himself, though married and lonesome for both his wife and the cultivated lifestyle they had developed together, is lucky to have no children and has "a good solid professional who's running the family business, and it continues to make money nicely in my absence." (MM, 104) He does not, then, yield to the typical instinct, for most people in the Styron universe, to consider himself the only one left out and, thus, indulge in all the Fortune-forcing activities that that can give rise to.

The other "corrective" to the narrator's sense of solitariness is Paul Marriott. The young novelist is confused by the contrast "between this spangled testimony to a career busily devoted to the arts of war and his worldly, cultivated manner. How, I wondered, had such a relatively young man lived a life so rich in military fulfillment yet had found the time to become expert in another language and, presumably, to develop a taste for the Finer Things?" (MM, 198) On various occasions they discuss Hemingway, Dreiser, Steegmuller's *Flaubert and Madame Bovary*, the merits of various of Flaubert's translators; and, when a reviewer bombards the narrator's first novel, it is Marriott who reminds him that the reviewer is probably both jealous and a mediocrity. Marriott speaks with such "firm, final authority in his reaction and his manner that it gave me tremendous heart." (MM, 208)

In contrast to the narrator, then, are the truly miserable, those who rank high on Dunlop's scale. The epitome is "Mr. Misery," Phil Santana, a professional golfer who was battered badly on Iwo Jima but returned to Cleveland to establish a successful golf shop, marry, and father three children. He had paid his dues and was deservedly collecting. Now, recalled to the Marines, he has had to sell his business and, since it will be irreplaceable, has been forced to sign on as a regular officer, for life. His own pains dulled by this, the narrator calls Santana's fate "just terrible," but Dunlop reminds him it is the "Fortunes of war." (MM, 196) While I do not think that Styron offers the historical resignation of Lacy Dunlop as a model of proper human response to life—to yield to the flow of history is to repeat the atrocities of the past in Styron's universe in the long run—Dunlop does manage to escape the tunnel vision of the Solitary and so has the potential to Transfer.

The narrator's critical confrontation in the story comes with the person who is neither cultivated nor perceptive nor miserable: the aggressive Darling P. Jeeter, Jr., "call me 'Dee'." In him Styron shows us the "Solitary in control," and Jeeter thus falls into the category of characters which contains Sophie's father, Lawyer Gray,

Colonel Templeton, and, at times, Helen Loftis, among others. He is the character so busy and so successfully realizing his promises at certain moments in his life that he has no sense of guilt with which to check his conduct.

Jeeter thunders into the narrator's solitary world, taking over the vacant half of the BOQ room which had theretofore been the hero's own. He shoves his record player onto a desktop full of novel proofsheets and turns it up to full pitch. His general bearing is one of "almost unprecedented loutishness" (MM, 202), and he speaks chipperly of his own Solitary vision: " 'What I really want to do is get over to Korea and stick about six inches of cold steel in as many of those God durned gooks I can get holt of'." (MM, 202) When he speaks of knife-fighting his gaze "mossed over with the glaze of arrested development." (MM, 204)

Jeeter shares a close relationship with his father, Gunner Jeeter, the block off which Dee has been chipped. They banter about war and drink and sex without restraint. But the Gunner is old now, a shadow of his former hell-raising, Jap-killing self; and he is terminally ill, dying finally in the narrator's care while the younger Jeeter is off in pursuit of other promises. Again the contrast of what one is or at least hopes to be to what one must ultimately become: "And at last I could only stand there helpless, delicately stroking his wasted old shoulders and murmuring foolish words of reassurance while the blood dribbled in vermillion runnels down the stringy arms, across the bruise-hued tattoo of the grand old Marine Corps globe-and-anchor embossed there God knew how many years ago during some whoring, celebrant shore leave in Seattle or Valparaiso or Shanghai, when those forearms, young and hard as whalebone, belonged to Stud Jeeter of the Horse Marines . . . ." (MM, 208)

It is perhaps in his reaction to old Jeeter that we see the narrator become aware of the subtleties of his own shortcomings. Jeeter was a strong, virile man, ever oblivious to the harm and visionlessness of his own blind commitment to the rituals of the Marine Corps. In a very real sense the narrator sees himself to be superior in that he would never yield to such bloodthirsty folderol. Yet he must reevaluate himself on two levels. First, because he detests both the man and, particularly, his son, he has tried to show them up, get ahead of them on Fortune's pecking order by manipulating the discussion, particularly of literature, to expose their lack of letters. Second, when he begins coughing all night, Stud Jeeter for the narrator is someone who must be disposed of: under the guise of concern for his health, the narrator advises young Jeeter to ship the old man to the hospital. When the son shows reluctance, the narrator orders him out. To quote Dee Jeeter, " 'Gettin' a tiny bit Asiatic, ain't you, old buddy? What's the matter, tryin' to pull rank on your old roomie?' " (MM, 208) However imprecise the terminology, Dee has a point. Once his father dies, he moves out, leaving the hero "free and solitary once more." (MM, 208)

On the second level, then, the narrator must assess the extent to which he is a flabby and untattooed Jeeter, contributing in subtler ways to the devastation of history, represented here by the Marines. Early in the story he accuses himself, in his blind acceptance of a Marine Corps reserve commission, of participating in the "witless acquiescence" (MM, 101) upon which Bismarck said the might of nations and bloody warfare were built. Sitting in a New York bar he can react with distaste to a nearby remark that " 'The Market's going to be in bad trouble if they de-escalate this war' " (MM, 102), but he goes without resistance nonetheless, yielding with contained bitterness to what he tacitly accepts as historical inevitability. Further on he recounts how, in his first stint with the Marines, he had efficiently taken part in the practice bombardment of an evacuated Negro settlement, a community in which half a dozen Negroes had earlier committed suicide rather than face removal. The irony of his own blind participation in the process is not lost on the present-day narrator, since "self-destruction . . . is rare among a race of people born to patiently endure their suffering." (MM, 103)

When, at the end of the present story, Marriott reveals himself to be a true Marine beneath the veneer of culture, the narrator must inevitably reflect on himself. While he does not "belong to the small elite fellowship to which [Marriott] belonged" (MM, 210), he shares with him and with his fellowship the blindness which such narrowings as "elitism" necessitate. If the Marines in this tale are "all wrapped up in their training manuals . . . and their dreams of advancement" (MM, 196), the narrator is equally involved in his of detached submersion in the world of humane letters. To get back to it as quickly as possible he will shut his mouth and do what the Corps orders.

I find the description and discussion of the Camp Lejeune officer's club emblematic of Styron's theme. Aglitter with swimming pool, "elephantine bar," and "pompous murals" which proclaim Marine Corps mythology, the narrator calls it a "cheap . . . simulacrum of a true elegance to be found in the outside world, and where one dared not utter a word against military life." (MM, 198) Officers clubs, here or elsewhere, are normally plush places where the strained warrior can regroup his nerve ends and succor his sensuality sufficiently to be on about the grizzly business of warfare once again the next day (to be back at "the club" again the next evening for more of the same). The analogy to the narrator is simply this: he has a career that he wishes to return to (his equivalent "club"), and he will do his dirty business to be allowed back there at the earliest possible moment.

It is perhaps worthy of an aside here that the essays Styron published in 1982 in *This Quiet Dust*[6] were virtually all written in the 1960s and early 1970s. On prison reform, American political conventions, American imperialism, we see the writer—at virtually the same moment he was creating the self-satisfied narrators of *Sophie's Choice* and "Marriott, the Marine"—attempting to involve himself in the necessary battle against human indignity, political corruption, blind obedience to ill-defined ideals, and even, in one famous essay, smoking. For this reason I must cite a statement made by the late John Gardner to which I initially took exception but which, now, seems to me quite perceptive. In referring to remarks late in *Sophie's Choice* which slur Irish policemen, Gardner remarks that we can see that Styron's attempts to get to the bottom of human injustice are all the more praiseworthy "because we know by his slips that they are not natural to him but earned."[7] The only word I would argue with is "slips": when Styron has Stingo say, for example, that in the crowd outside the Pink Palace on the occasion of Sophie's and Nathan's suicides, "everywhere stood clots of thuggish [Irish] policemen chewing gum and negligently swatting their thick behinds" (*SC*, 506–7), he is *not* the present-day Styron *slipping*; rather he is the 1947 Stingo-Styron speaking as he might have in those days. Both *Sophie's Choice* and "Marriott the Marine" are stories which show Styron (as Stingo or the unnamed author) becoming aware of his own participation in human evil. They are contemporary in their composition, and they are the only two works we have in which the first-person narrator is not pointedly identifiable as some one other than William Styron.

Because "Marriott, the Marine" is only the beginning of a novel, we see little yet of the final four themes which I have been discussing: Fortune-forcing, God, Lying, and Transfer. In most Styron works these enter later, after the first four are thoroughly established and destructively operating. We do have one very standard early-novel statement on God: in drawing an extended analogy the narrator remarks on the "benighted city of Villahermosa . . . where even priests went mad with the heat and died railing at a deity heartless enough to create this inferno on earth." (MM, 202) In terms of lying, we get the standard amount of alcoholic oblivion to get over a spate of ill Fortune which ranges from reinduction into the Marines to bad book reviews. With regard to Transfer, however, the dimension most thoroughly developed in this story's contemporary counterpart, *Sophie's Choice*, we can see the seeds being planted even as far along as the story is. There is Lacy's instruction on being aware of the misery of others as well as one's own. Marriott recognizes that Marine infantrymen are not as well fed as he is and ought to be better served. Even the narrator can feel fundamentally shaken by the death of old Jeeter whom he had despised. But the clearest example of the concept is the reference to the Whitehurst store sign the narrator had found after he and his cronies had blissfully bombarded the vacated Negro settlement. Because of its crucial place in fixing the thematic position of the later Styron, I will quote this section at length:

> And I recalled feeling then a small tug at my heart, not for any damage done to an already ruined hulk, nor even out of conscience, but because Whitehurst was the name of my father's mother, whose family had lived here on this Carolina coast for two centuries and had owned Negroes who bore the Whitehurst name. Thus this store-keeper had most certainly been descended from slaves owned by my

ancestors—could it be that he was one of those who sought suicide in his grief? I never found out—and as I stood on that smoking ruin with its intermingled fragrance of gunpowder and honeysuckle I could not help but feel a pang of morbid regret over the fact that it was I who had presided so efficiently at the obliteration of a place one Whitehurst must have once cherished dearly. It seemed oddly gratuitous on my part, and something of an insult. (MM, 103)

Turning to Styron's first Marine Corps story, written two decades earlier, these same themes can again be seen in a much less developed form; but they are present nonetheless. Stingo refers to it as a "taut, searing book eviscerating the military in a tragicomedy of the absurd" (*SC*, 450), and this is the line of approach many critics have pursued as they celebrate Styron's "first political gesture as a man of letters."[8] While I have no argument with that sort of approach, other than that it is too narrow given the matters *Sophie's Choice* has called attention to, I would rather examine the book as a paradigm for the man/man and man/God relationships we have been examining in Styron's other work.

Roger Asselineau has universalized the story by claiming that Styron, far beyond the confines of the Marine Corps, is demonstrating that "life is an interminable forced march in the night."[9] As such it takes on certain allegorical dimensions which, if they should not be pushed too far, should at least be acknowledged. This has been done, frequently. Irving Malin has pointed out that Captain Mannix's first word in the story is "Jesus,"[10] and Wayne Carver has labeled Mannix "a rebellious Christ."[11] Peter Hays has studied the religious implications of *The Long March*;[12] and Eugene McNamara, in one of the earliest critical examinations of this novella, has seen Mannix as the Old Adam and Satan, Templeton as a "priest," and Culver as the potential convert.[13] Recognizing all this, I would like to simplify the discussion here by suggesting that, on one level at least, Templeton is a God-figure (as his name possibly indicates) and that Mannix is recalcitrant mankind, "nix-Man" as Maxwell Geismar has claimed.[14] Templeton runs the show in this story, and Mannix is an unwilling, later rebellious participant in it.

It is a show made up of two main acts: the accidental killing of eight recruits by a short-fired shell and the thirty-six mile forced march of a flabby, middle-aged battalion whom Templeton suspects of "doping off." Like "Marriott, the Marine" the story takes place in 1951 amidst the resentment of reserve officers who have gone along with historical absurdity through one unasked-for war and now must, a brief six years later, endure yet another one that is even more pointless and less defined. Richard Pearce pinions the situation cleanly when he says this is a world in which "man is surprised, ambushed, senselessly assaulted—not to the end of defeat or destruction, not to any end at all."[15] As a consequence we have the Styron Solitaries showing up immediately—Templeton who has found an amoral role in an amoral situation; Mannix who recognizes the amorality and makes a personal (not a universal, humanitarian, nor even symbolic) gesture against it; and Culver, the eyes of the reader, who is ultimately trapped between them. In the terms I have been pursuing, Culver is the historical victim caught between those who make use of the world as it is for their own benefit (Hitler, McBride, Mason Flagg, Darling P. Jeeter) and those who would have it be otherwise for theirs (Nat, Milton Loftis, Cass Kinsolving, and at times Stingo).

The opening of *The Long March* is similar to all Styron's openings up to *Sophie's Choice*: the emphasis is on loss, on something that happened which is the dead opposite of what "should have" happened. In short, the Promise/Realization theme once again. (In Styron's most recent novel the emphasis shifts to Stingo who is glibly in charge and must later be undercut.) Other than the addition of real instead of anticipated violence, the situation parallels "Marriott, the Marine" almost as exactly as the narrator of that story had cautioned that it might: the almost dream-like quality the years between 1945 and 1950 assume in retrospect, the return of two of Fortune's darlings to the bottom of the Wheel, the bitterness against both the world for producing another war and the self for accepting a disguised invitation some years back to participate. During the short course of *The Long March* Culver and Mannix learn, among other things, that the world beyond the military (which they had taken to be just realization of earlier promises) is really a child's vision and that they, as all human beings, are "lost in the night, astray at mid-century in the never-endingness of war." (*LM*, 82)[16] In allegorical terms which parallel the God references we have seen in other novels, man (Mannix) will say no to such a Divine Plan (as represented by Templeton), curse it in familiar Styronian terms (" 'Who cares what you think. . . . *Fuck* you and your information.' " [*LM*, 62, 77]), then bemoan his fate once the cursing and rebellion collapse into pointlessness (" 'Won't they ever let us alone?' " [*LM*, 43]). Mannix speaks all these lines, as he does the final line of the hike which only the most gullible reader could take literally: having finished the march and stumbled back into camp, he says in self-deluding triumph to Culver " 'What the hell . . . we've made it.' " (*LM*, 79)

One thing which critics have rightly mentioned from the start is that Mannix is an ambiguous hero whose actions are frequently self-canceling. August Nigro summarizes this character flaw by saying of Mannix that "the pride and will that move him to rebellion are also the tragic flaws that bind him to his own tyranny."[17] Stated in my terms, Mannix, in the sense of being ill-used by Fortune (as surely he is and Nat and Sophie were as well), resorts to the most flagrant sort of Fortune-forcing that we see in any Styron novel: he assists the God-figure in actuating His "misguided design" in order to prove that he can survive this design and be God's equal or even better in doing so. In terms of the story, Mannix will take those who are victims as he is and compel them at all cost to complete their roles as victims by suffering the fullest atrocities of Fortune. In so doing he alone can assure himself of his manhood and his ability to control Fortune and its aberrations. He loses his sense of guilt and so participates in Evil. Culver realizes this by the end of the novella when he says, in his plea to Mannix's humanity, " 'let's face it, you don't really care if they make it. You. Me, maybe. But these guys . . . anybody else. What the hell.' " (*LM*, 55–56) To another such plea Mannix says, simply, " 'To hell with them all.' " (*LM*, 74) And he goes on to finish it himself, with Culver and a few others hobbling in tow.

Throughout Styron's work this has been the pattern of human evil: in recognizing the injustice of Fortune, man generally reacts in such a way as to play Fortune's dirty game, attempting to shift the perceived abuse from his own shoulders to those "beneath" him. In the scene in which Mannix tells the training officer that he does not know the answers to the questions being asked at the lecture, Culver recognizes that "far from giving the impression that he had been purged, that he had blown off excess pressure, he seemed instead more tense, more embittered, more in need to scourge something—his own boiling spirit, authority, anything." (*LM*, 35) It is on the forced march that we ultimately see him get his scourging done, threatening his men with retribution if they fail to prove they are up to Templeton's guiltless demands. What he seeks from them is what he has built in himself, "proud and willful submission, rebellion in reverse." (*LM*, 50) Eventually, miles down the North Carolina road (and allegorically miles down the road of life), Mannix has become "involved in something routine, an act in which his brain, long past cooperation, played hardly any part at all." (*LM*, 53) I think there is no better brief statement anywhere in Styron to summarize the human race, collectively and individually, and its participation in the course of history. The individual resents that course but helps it along to squeeze something for himself or herself from it. It becomes necessary that he or she literally "enslave" other people: "Panic-stricken, limping with blisters and with exhaustion, and in mutinous despair, the men fled westward, whipped on by Mannix's cries." (*LM*, 68)

In the midst of Mannix's forcing of Fortune, Culver can see exactly what he is trying to do, but he lacks the moral fortitude to try effectively to prevent him. Trapped in escapist dreams, he feels "adrift at sea in a dazzling windowless box" (*LM*, 23); he is frustrated that he is no better than a cooperative victim in this process, be it long march or life, "that he was not independent enough, nor possessed of enough free will, was not *man* enough to say to hell with it and crap out himself." (*LM*, 71) Unlike Mannix he can recognize that the struggle "is simply no longer worth the effort" (*LM*, 76), but that is as much as he is able to contribute. The evil goes on about him as if he did not exist.

I would like to discuss now the matter of Templeton as a God-figure in this novel. Once again we are confronted with the question, asked in every Styron book, as to God's ill-will, misplanning, lack of the charity in dealing with man that the New Testament suggests is God's central demand of mankind. If Styron is seeking a one-to-one equation here, the blame, as it always *seems* to be, is squarely on God's shoulders. Templeton is unemotional, demanding, sadistic, threatening, yet ultimately involved in a situation he seems not up to—he perhaps cannot do himself what he requires his men to do but demands their subservience nonetheless. If he can inspire blind loyalty in a toady such as O'Leary, he inspires anger and hatred in almost everyone else. In the long run he sets them at each other's throats. This is the paradigm of God and His universe that is cursed by Sophie, Stingo, Cass, Peyton, and—here—Mannix.

Yet *is* this Styron on God, or Styron on man's misapprehended conception of God? Consider this description of Templeton: "In men like Templeton all emotion—all smiles, all anger—emanated from a priestlike, religious fervor, throbbing inwardly with the cadence of parades and booted footfalls. By that passion rebels are ordered into quick damnation but simple doubters sometimes find indulgence—depending upon the priest, who may be one inclined toward mercy, or who is one ever rapt in some litany of punishment and court-martial." (*LM*, 20) He goes on to say that Templeton is "devout but inclined toward mercy." Here, then, seems to be man's problem with God which we have seen in other forms in other works. On the one hand God, or a Marine colonel, represents authority in that he must demand that some "proper" standard be met, to an extent a sacrifice of each of our human liberties to do what we damn well please. Al Mannix simply cannot be Al Mannix all the way up in this, or probably any, social situation. On the other hand Templeton and God represent protection and mercy— love, perhaps—and this leads man to expect treatment he perhaps cannot have and dare not expect. God as standard-setter and God as favor-dispenser clash in man's mind, especially when the former role seems so much more in evidence than the latter. In man's tendency to establish egocentric universes, the disparity is further compounded, the resentment against God or Colonel grows, "rebellion in reverse" results.

Now, consider the same point from the position of Templeton-as-man rather than Templeton as God-figure. Templeton like all men is egocentric—feels he can decipher the "divine plan," or at least the version of it which best suits his needs as the Solitary in quest of Fortune's rewards; and so—virtually in the name of God or morality or at least common sense—he commences to enforce his will, which he mistakes to be God's will (*mendacity* I have heard this termed and it is a good word) upon those "beneath him." In military terms it is his batallion; in human terms it is everybody, for he even violates the regulations for marching which have been given to him by those above him.

In summary, then, Templeton is performing as God as he perceives God himself to perform, and he is seen by his men to be doing so also. As in all the other works, then, Styron's argument is not with God—his interviews suggest strong agnosticism anyway—but with the individual's perception of God on the one hand and his or her inclination to act as God on the other. The reason why people act as God is always because most people's universes are egocentric, and in them they crave the omnipotence they perceive themselves to deserve.

What do we make then of Templeton's concern for Mannix's injured foot? Marc Ratner claims that "when the Colonel stops to examine Mannix's wound, Culver sees Templeton's total lack of humanity. Culver then realizes that Templeton is as indifferent as the universe to man's pain."[18] A number of other critics, faithful to Styron's indictment of the Marines, agree with him. Yet, while it might be said that Templeton has proven his point and had never really intended to push for the entire thirty-six miles once he had brought his men to their knees, this does not seem to me to be Styron's own point. Rather there seems to be a sharp contrast being drawn between the monomaniacal Mannix and the chastened Templeton. Mannix keeps thinking of the eight dead soldiers, seems almost to be compelling himself and his men on the march out of duty to their spirits and memories, almost "winning it for the Gipper." Templeton has set out to pace the march, found himself in pain, perhaps has begun to feel some shame and guilt for what he has concocted. In any event, when he orders Mannix onto the truck, he is making more sense than Mannix who refuses to allow himself or his men to quit. Styron's complaint, and Culver's, with the Colonel's gesture is, first, that it is out of place given the climate the Colonel has established; and, second and by corollary, it is too late.

The damage to body and spirit has already been done, as well as the damage to the human soul which will allow man to do evil in retaliation. This act of Transfer becomes as ironically ridiculous as Faulkner's Flem Snopes presenting Mrs. Armstid with a packet of candy after the spotted horses fiasco nearly killed her husband.

Other than Culver's plea for mercy for the bedraggled company, of which he is one, the only other act approaching Transfer in the story is set, as it usually is, in the final pages and, typical of the early Styron, in a scene dominated by a Negro character. When the maid in the BOQ says to the almost-naked Mannix " 'Oh my, you poor man. What you been doin'? Do it hurt?. . . Oh, I bet it does. 'Deed it does.' " (*LM*, 83), they share "one unspoken moment of sympathy and understanding." This instinctive recognition of a fellow mortal's pain is what Templeton and Mannix, each for his own reason, could not command at the moments they needed to. As Mannix stands naked before the maid, a cake of soap in his hand, we are given, I think, a simple moment of cleansing through unity: a new understanding that the world unfortunately cannot be what Mannix would like it to be or even what Culver dreams about, but that it could be better than man has allowed it to be.

But Mannix has "endured and lasted" (*LM*, 84) and perhaps can perform differently another day. He has survived both the illogic of the Marines and the illogic of his "rebellion in reverse," both of which create evil. In the clash of these two Solitary men, Mannix and Templeton, perhaps potential good has been born.[19]

Notes

1. "Marriott, the Marine," *Esquire,* September, 1971, pp. 101–4, 196, 198, 200, 202, 204, 207–8, 210.

2. Forkner, pp. 923–34.

3. Forkner, p. 929.

4. Forkner, p. 929.

5. All page numbers refer to the 1971 *Esquire* version, n. 1 above.

6. *This Quiet Dust* (New York, Random House, 1982).

7. John Gardner, "A Novel of Evil," *The New York Times Book Review*, May 27, 1979, p. 17.

8. Melvin Friedman, *William Styron* (Bowling Green, Ohio: Bowling Green University Popular Press, 1974), p. 40.

9. Roger Asselineau, "*En Suivant* La marche de nuit *de William Styron*," *La Revue Des Lettres Modernes*, Nos. 157–171 (1967), 73–83.

10. Irving Malin, "The Symbolic March," in Morris and Malin, p. 124.

11. Wayne Carver, "The Grand Inquisitor's Long March," *University of Denver Quarterly*, 1 (1966), 37–64.

12. Peter L. Hays, "The Nature of Rebellion in *The Long March*," *Critique*, 8 (1965–66), 70–74.

13. Eugene McNamara, "William Styron's *Long March*: Absurdity and Authority," *Western Humanities Review*, 15 (1961), 267–72.

14. Maxwell Geismar, *American Moderns: From Rebellion to Conformity* (New York: Hill and Wang, 1958), p. 248.

15. Richard Pearce, *William Styron*, UMPAW 98 (Minneapolis: University of Minnesota Press, 1971), p. 20.

16. *The Long March* (New York: Vintage Books, 1952). All page numbers refer to this edition.

17. August Nigro, "*The Long March*: The Expansive Hero in a Closed World," *Critique*, 9 (1967), 103–12.

18. Marc L. Ratner, *William Styron* (New York: Twayne Publishers, 1972), p. 66.

19. Styron has also written a play about the Marines, *In the Clap Shack* (1973). Though the same distaste for his military experiences is clearly evident, I do not think it fits cleanly into the matters he treats in his two pieces of military fiction. The play concerns the ineptitude of various military hospital personnel who misdiagnose the hero's medical problems and convince him that he has contracted syphilis. In a sense there is a reversal of the Promise/Realization theme here when the hero discovers in the end that he does not have syphilis at all, but on the whole I do not think that Styron's single attempt at becoming a playwright is consistent with his fictional interests in a larger context.

4

ENSLAVED IN
ANOTHER'S MICROCOSM
Lie Down in Darkness

In *Lie Down in Darkness,* Styron's first novel, the birth of the themes I have been discussing, or most of them at least, occurs in the first two chapters. Yet, since these are the first two chapters of Styron's entire literary canon, the author could not have suspected, I am sure, the degree to which these concerns would become the thematic earmark of his art. When Ben Forkner and Gilbert Schricke interviewed Styron in France in 1974, they asked him to comment on the thematic relation of the novel upon which he was currently working (*Sophie's Choice*) to the one which had launched his career.

BEN FORKNER: Is there any connection between the themes you were struggling with in *Lie Down in Darkness* and the process of learning Sophie's story and the development of your relationship with her?

WILLIAM STYRON: Yes, that's important and I should emphasize that because part of the story is that of the young kid who's desperately yearning to write. He wants to write so bad his teeth ache. He wants to publish, he knows he has something churning in him, about a family in the South and about the death of a girl. And incidentally, his father sends him a clipping ("him" being of course I, the narrator, whatever you want to call him) about the death of a girl who kills herself in New York. This girl, the narrator realizes, was the same girl he was in love with some years before and consequently this starts other things churning in his head because he realizes that his novel could have the theme of a girl who commits suicide in New York and is sent to Potter's Field and is buried. And all these things begin to percolate in his head, but he has an impossible time putting it down on paper for reasons he is not really aware of yet, of course, simply due to the fact that—I hate to cast it in this terrible cliche but I will: *he has not experienced enough.* At least he has not seen enough of life, so that the events of the summer of his love for this girl and her tormented relationship with him and Nathan and their eventual deaths, *enable him to apprehend things, to be able to start to write.* It's a catalytic event or series of events which give him self knowledge at the very end and which enable him, as the reader I presume will see, to go on and write a book which has not been called *Lie Down in Darkness* but will be called *Lie Down in Darkness.*[1] [Italics mine]

I hope to show that Styron-Stingo's experiences with Sophie, which he did not commit to paper for almost thirty more years, were at least subliminally understood enough to become the moral center of his first novel, if not—yet—for a story of Auschwitz which is "horrible beyond belief."[2] In fact, Stingo is embarrassed to have to admit, at one point in *Sophie's Choice,* that he got a lucky break in having Maria Hunt (Peyton Loftis) die so that he would have a subject to write about.

The theme of loneliness—or solitariness as I have been calling it—is immediately evident at the novel's outset. The four central characters are approaching Peyton's burial in two pairs: Milton Loftis and Dolly Bonner, Helen Loftis and Carey Carr. Peyton's body is not even escorted on the train to Port Warwick, and this immediately emphasizes her solitariness, the full dimension of which we will not understand until her interior monologue begins in the book's final chapter. Yet the other four are as alone as she is. Milton has asked Dolly to accompany him so he *won't* be alone; but, as she sits beside him in the limousine, he tries his best to ignore her, tacitly wishes she would shut up, and eventually betakes himself to a diner to get away from her and so be alone with his grief and self-pity. Dolly, of course, realizes not only this but also that Milton will now leave her for good, even to the extent of begging Helen to have him back as a husband once again. Later Carey Carr, whom we first see driving over to escort Helen to the funeral, does not know what to say to her and has long ago decided not only that she is unreachable, perhaps even mad, but also that he has no counsel to give in the first place. Helen has simply felt "enveloped by loneliness" for as long as she can remember.

The present time of this novel lasts only a few hours—the time it takes to transport Peyton's body from the railway station to the cemetery. In those few hours we are given five separate individuals for whom the whole battle with Fortune is over. The five are isolated in an intolerable present of unrealized promises. Since all their promises were necessarily different from the start, they are not able to console each other at all at the moment of their common loss.

Milton

Several critics have recognized the seedlings of the promise-realization theme in the lives of the characters in *Lie Down in Darkness*, though they discuss it in different terminology. Ihab Hassan, for example, feels that "Milton Loftis, his wife Helen, and their daughter Peyton are all locked in a domestic tragedy in which love must wear the face of guilt and the *search for childhood innocence* must acquaint the seeker with death."[3] Marc L. Ratner says that the book "is essentially a tragedy of character, not of Fate"[4] because the central characters are trying to "fulfill their desires by reliving their youths in the lives of their children."[5] Stated in our present terms, they will attempt vicariously to relive the promises of their own youths, this time to have things turn out "right."

Milton Loftis is essentially a determinist, indeed feels more comfortable in a world of inevitability in that it deprives him of moral responsibility for the unrealized promises. Although we see him in the first chapter trying to think solely of the *now*, he knows that he cannot confine time to the present, "that the train would come after all, bringing with it the final proof of fate and circumstance." (*LDD*, 14)[6]

As in most of Styron's writing, the primary shaper of the child is the father, and Milton's upbringing is no exception—" 'you must tread a long narrow path toward your destiny. If the crazy sideroads start to beguile you, son, take at least a backward glance at Monticello.' " (*LDD*, 74) What Milton misses in his father's guidance, however, is the suggestion of free will despite the heavy emphasis on Fate, the difference from the "sophomoric fatalism" he, at another moment, cautions Milton to avoid. Indeed, by the day of Peyton's funeral Milton "despised his father" (*LDD*, 17) because "his father lacked the foresight to avoid spoiling his son and to realize that sending him to the University . . . would produce the results it did." (*LDD*, 15) Yet the longer Milton reflects on his father this doom-laden day, the more he must admit that he "had never taken his advice seriously, . . . those warnings . . . he had shrugged off quickly, although with a vague feeling of resentment, perhaps because he sensed they might come true." (*LDD*, 45) Milton, in short, is seeking one of two scapegoats for the unrealized promise: either his father for spoiling him despite the warnings or Fortune for constructing a system in which the warnings were gratuitous in the first place.

What then did Fortune seem to offer Milton and then not relinquish to him? The most obvious is a happy marriage when he won the colonel's daughter, a beauty whom even his own cautious father had highly approved of. Instead, he has a jealous, pietistic, neurotic, religion-chilled woman who does not even sleep in his bed. Another is his political aspirations which, in his fantasies, had taken him as high as the presidency. Though he sharply reduced his expectations over the next twenty years, as low as Commonwealth's attorney, he has instead wound up with nothing and become "a goddam rotten failure, a bloodsucker using my wife's money to get just a little bit ahead, by which I mean to keep as well-stocked with bourbon as the next hot shot in town. . . ." (*LDD*, 88) Attached to these are general frustrations such as lost youth and the failure of such ingrained gentlemanly ideals as one "didn't go around making love to a woman you weren't married to, in your own house." (*LDD*, 178) There is even disillusionment with the failure of America to realize her promises—a major theme in Styron's next work, *Set This House on Fire*. To quote Milton's father: "We lost our lovewords. Not the South or the North, or any of those old things. 'S the U.S.A. We've gone to pot. It's a stupid war but the next one'll be stupider, and then we'll like my father said stand on the last reef of time and look up into the night and breathe the stench of the awful enfolding shroud.'" (*LDD*, 185–186)

To counter his middle-aged predicament, Milton indulges in Fortune-forcing in two major ways. Most obviously he takes Dolly Bonner as his mistress, a woman whom he does not love but who serves his purposes—whether simply as a friend to fill his loneliness, a vessel for sexual release, or (once Helen discovers it) a retaliation against his wife for what she turned out to be. The other means by which he attempts to force Fortune and so cause the greatest ruination of his promise is the appropriation of Peyton as a surrogate wife and a surrogate self.

I think the following lines are emblematic of Milton's misuse of Peyton's adolescent years and suggest the reasons for his eventual moral collapse and her suicide:

> The door of the room where they stood, he and Peyton together, her hand in his, confronted the edge of darkness, like a shore at night facing on the sea. Beyond them in the shadows arose swollen, mysterious scents, powders and perfumes which, though familiar to both of them, never lost the odor of strangeness and secrecy—to him because they stung his senses with memories of dances and parties in the distant past, and of love, always the scent of gardenias. In Peyton they aroused wicked excitement, a promise, too, of dances and parties, and—since she was still nine years old—hope that when the Prince came finally with love and a joyful rattling of spurs, the day would smell like this, a heartbreaking scent, always of roses. (*LDD*, 63)

In this passage we can clearly see the Electra complex and the latent incest that can only lead to mutual frustration. Milton can never resist physical contact with her, buys her a ring on the very day he learns that Dick has given her his pin, and pursues her through football crowds and fraternity frivolity in the very hours his other daughter, Maudie, is giving up her life.

It is not simply the accidents of their births, that Peyton had to be his daughter and so beyond his reach, which destroy the promise Milton has unwittingly made to himself; it is also the passage of time. On her wedding day he conjures up moments of happiness in her youth that they had shared together, only to have them interrupted by the reality of the occasion at hand: "*Time! Time!* he thinks. *My God, has it finally come to this, do I finally know?* And lost in memory, thinking not of Peyton but of this final knowledge—this irrevocable loss of her. . . ." (*LDD*, 289) Because of the expectations they had for life—Milton's manufactured out of an attempt to start his life over and have it run properly, Peyton's from the misdirection provided by both her father and her mother—neither is able to live within the terms of existence as they actually can be. Even on the day of her burial he is able to couple his desperate remark ("'This is the worst thing that ever happened to me'") to an equally desperate thought which suggests that, even in the face of death, Milton (and mankind in Styron's universe) still thinks that a right action on his part will undo the past and redirect Fortune to its proper course. "Is not just remorse enough? Isn't there a way to set all this right? Isn't this grief enough? How long? What can I do?" (*LDD*, 45)

Although the themes I have been discussing are not as sharply drawn in *Lie Down in Darkness* as they will be in *The Confessions of Nat Turner* and in *Sophie's Choice*, Milton Loftis is nonetheless the first Styron hero to run the gamut of them: from locking himself into a solitary vision of existence in which Fortune will cooperatively allow the promises Milton has made to himself to be realized, to a blatant, egocentric attempt to set things aright, to foolish fabrications about life when that attempt proves fruitless. Dolly, Peyton, liquor—for Milton all were "props and crutches . . . which supported him against the unthinkable notion that life was not rich and purposeful and full of rewards." (*LDD*, 43) On the day of Peyton's burial, Milton tries again to force the terms of his life into some imagined order: first he begs Helen to take him back and, when she rejects him, he lunges at her and tries to strangle her to death, screaming "'God damn you! . . . If I can't have . . . then you . . . nothing! . . . Die, damn you, die!'" (*LDD*, 388)

Helen

Helen Loftis is an example in Styron's world of the sort of person who feels that he or she has identified God's will and is fully prepared to perform as He desires. Any resistance he or she meets is seen, not only as an offense against oneself and his or her personal promises, but also an offense against the teleological Divine Plan. Hence, all Fortune-forcing to realize unkept promises is clothed in righteousness; but here again Styron insists that the Will of God is certainly not very available to most men—surely it is not to Carey Carr who has searched hard for it—and so we are shown a differently-disguised Solitary who is not exempt from the pattern of human behavior I have been examining in Styron's work.

Carr says of Helen that she "was a woman who had not been the dupe of life, but had been too selfish, too unwilling to make the usual compromises, to be happy." (*LDD*, 126) A person unwilling to make any compromises with life is most surely to suffer the torture of unrealized promises even more than most other men. Note Helen's self-assessment of her life:

> One has no idea what it is to stand by quietly and watch those bricks you've so carefully put together . . . crumble away, begin to topple off. It starts so slowly, takes you by surprise and sneaks up on you a little more month by month until then, at one point, you look around and discover that this whole structure you've so carefully built—and not yet completed—has begun to dissolve like sand in water . . . so that you want to throw a cloak over the whole mess . . . and then, later wanting . . . by some shrewd decorous masonry to repair, repair, saying, "Oh, please stop, please stop," all the while. (*LDD*, 115)

As she, Milton, and Peyton sit together in the Charlottesville hospital to await the doctor's word on Maudie, she laments " 'I have waited all my life, it seems, for things to happen, for things to come that never came. . . .' " (*LDD*, 217) Since she sees her own will to be aligned with the deity's, she can easily moralize in her own favor anytime she confronts her husband or younger daughter. When at the finale of Peyton's wedding she scolds her for her treatment of her father, who is currently in Helen's favor, the emphasis is always on the first person singular: " 'After all I've planned. After everything I've tried . . . I'll forget . . . I'll overlook. . . .' " (*LDD*, 311) When Milton tries to find his way back to her after Maudie's death, she thankfully, almost gleefully tells him " 'Oh my darling, you do understand me, after all. . . . Darling, you have learned, haven't you? You have learned what I need, haven't you? . . . Oh, yes together we can never die!'" (*LDD*, 256) (To the extent that Milton serves her needs he will apparently become immortal, just as God has told man that immortality in heaven comes from serving His!) For Milton, however, full entry into a Helen-centered universe is little short of emasculation: "'. . . what have you wanted from me, my manhood guts and balls and soul? What in Christ's name have you wanted? I've offered you everything I've got—.'" (*LDD*, 255)

In clinging so uncompromisingly to her solitary vision of what life should be, she has become a grotesque of the sort Sherwood Anderson portrays in *Winesburg, Ohio*. For Milton, "her hair is getting grey, her face pinched with bitterness, or religion." (*LDD*, 153) Earlier, as he escorts Peyton up to Helen's room to apologize for tying Maudie up, he thinks "What has happened to those warm, loving hands which once took care of us so well?" (*LDD*, 64)

Marc Ratner has called Milton "a case of arrested development,"[7] but I think it is wrong to stop the list of such cases in Styron's first novel at one alone. Even though Helen can recognize that she and Milton once loved each other because "they were both still young and hadn't had to grow up to things" (*LDD*, 31), it does not seem to me that she has grown up herself. More to the point, then, might be Maxwell Geismar's comment that "the true theme of the novel—all its tenderness and tragedy—lies in the evocation of that childhood world of illusion where all our feelings were direct and full and complete."[8] The childhood world of illusion is greatly comprised of the promises each man expects to be realized with the onset of that omnipotent moment in one's life called young adulthood. With the non-realization comes a middle age of disillusionment and despair but, before that, the attempt to at least pretend that things have taken shape pretty much as they were supposed to. Helen can tell Carey, but more important can tell herself, that she and Peyton had " 'had so much fun, really, packing and all and getting excited together about going off to school. . . .' " (*LDD*, 116) This is the way her childhood dream of mother-daughter relationships should be, and she is desperate to recreate the feeling she had had when, only twenty-four, she thought "she could go on being a mother forever." (*LDD*, 30) Later she falsifies her true feelings and lures Peyton home for her wedding: "Anything that people should know Helen Loftis was a good mother, a successful mother. Anything that people should know: it was Helen Loftis, that suffering woman, who had brought together the broken family." (*LDD*, 274)

In the midst of the shambles of middle age, as we have seen in the two previous novels I have discussed, the subject of the role of God in all this inevitably arises. Despite her apparent religiosity, Helen's position on God is very similar to those Styron would repeat in the minds and words of the main characters in *The Confessions of Nat Turner* and *Sophie's Choice*. Helen has the sense of God abandoning her at key moments in her life: after Maudie's death "her prayers seemed to be on a one-way line to heaven." (*LDD*, 132) When she tries to revive His presence in her life she finds that "God . . . was beyond reflection, like trying to picture your remotest ancestor." (*LDD*, 140) In an exchange very reminiscent of the other novels, she tells Carey Carr that she did not desert God, but " 'God deserted me . . . When Maudie died.' " (*LDD*, 238) As we have seen before, such a statement from the mouth of a Styron character generally means that God has failed to create a Helen-centered universe, has not seen fit to make the Divine Will conform to hers. An interesting difference in Helen's case, however, is this: whereas Nat and Stingo and perhaps Sophie pause to reflect that God may have "deserted" them (and mankind) in disappointment and disgust, no such re-evaluation of self is possible for Helen. Rather, in returning to Milton after Maudie's death, she creates her own God *in him*, which, given his full submission to her ("guts and balls and soul"), is the very sort of God she and other Styron malcontents require. "Didn't he [Carey] know she had found her God? Didn't he know that the devil had been slain, that Milton was her Prince of Light, come back all virtuous after befouling himself. . . . She, Helen, had raised him up, re-formed him in the image of decency, exalted him." (*LDD*, 294)

Helen alone among Styron's major characters will remain both alive and thoroughly unchastened at the end of her novel, which perhaps explains Milton's final melodramatic attempt to strangle her.

Peyton

It does not need mentioning that a beautiful twenty-two-year-old young woman who takes her own life and is buried anonymously in a Potter's Field is an easy symbol for unrealized promise. Yet the retrieval of her remains and reburial of them among the fragments of a broken family, the family which pointed her toward her demise, is the framing principle of *Lie Down in Darkness*. By extension, it is the first indication of the central predicament of Styron's entire canon: ruination of one's own existence by following the misguided directives of the past.

If the promise/realization theme in itself represents a dichotomy, Peyton is probably more torn by that dichotomy than any other character Styron has yet created. This is simply because she is expected to live by two starkly different standards, that is, to realize two diametrically opposed promises. Since this cannot be done by any human being she is doomed from the start to failure; and, since those two sharply-defined standards have been so repeatedly made clear to her, she has small space left within her mind and soul in which to identify and explore the one, surely different from either, which she should properly set for herself.

What does Milton expect her to become? First of all, she is the perfectly-formed daughter who alleviated his doubt and guilt after the malformed Maudie became his first born. In this way, she must realize all the benefits of her fortunate birth: boys, parties, clothes, "proper" schooling, well-born husband. The "great moments" of her life will have to be staged public occasions—her sixteenth birthday, her return from school each Christmas, her wedding. As he tells her more than once "'When you grow up, baby, . . . you're going to be wonderful.'" (*LDD*, 67) As a consequence, Milton overdoes everything from feeding her whiskey at sixteen to staging a wedding which can only turn into bedlam.

On the other hand, however, he needs Peyton as a surrogate lover. He forces as much physical contact with her as he dares, hangs on as long as possible to watch her undress, seeks her out for the counsel a man "normally" married would seek from his wife, has her call him "Bunny" as a girlfriend might, gives her tokens of his affection to balance the ones given her by potential beaus. In so doing he has created a love in response which is not entirely healthy for Peyton's development, has set askew her abilities to seek what she needs from all the males who pursue her, and has created a sense of guilt and perverted responsibility in her which too often places his warped needs ahead of her own best interests.

Helen's "needs" with regard to Peyton could not be more opposite. In her great attachment to her retarded first-born daughter she almost sees Peyton as a cruel joke played against Maudie. As a result anything Peyton experiences that might be called "normal" for a young girl is disparaged and criticized simply because Maudie cannot be normal. Beauty, intelligence, sexuality, vibrancy, and *joie de vivre*—all are vices in Peyton because they are out of Maudie's reach. Peyton, in Helen's darkest moments, is ironically a realized promise which by contrast exposes a terribly unrealized one. Even though Peyton and Maudie seem quite fond of each other, Helen tries to separate them as much as possible, perhaps to punish Peyton for being who and what she is, perhaps to shield Maudie from the comparison, perhaps to deprive Peyton of giving the love to others which is an essential part of her being. The comparison of her with Caddy Compson is a meaningful analogy here, I think, as is a further extension of that analogy to Helen and Caroline Compson. Ultimately, Peyton even errs in such a way that Helen can see her as having "killed" Maudie.

Whenever we watch Peyton acting on her own we get the sense of someone on stage, being observed by hostile critics; and after her performances she frequently drops into despair. In the final letter she writes to Milton before her suicide, she says "Oh, Daddy, I don't know what's wrong. I've tried to grow up—to be a good little girl as you would say, but everywhere I turn I seem to walk deeper and deeper into some terrible despair. . . . What have we done with our lives so that everywhere we turn—no matter how hard we try not to—we cause other people sorrow? (*LDD*, 38) In the terms of Styron's reading of the world, the broad answer to this question is that none of us is likely to want, or even be able, to play the role we must to satisfy the vision of whichever Solitary is currently regarding us. Unless, that is, we are reduced to the level of Negro slave, of fawning toady (Cass Kinsolving), or of Auschwitz inmate. In terms more pointed at Peyton's difficulty, she has two parents who "expect" opposite behavior from her, she has not been able to discover who she is and where she fits in her world, and hence she becomes a wanderer who tantalizes and frustrates virtually everyone with whom she makes contact, whether husband or lover or innocent bystander. " 'I've wanted to be normal. I've wanted to be like everybody else' " (*LDD*, 268), she cries in frustration.

Perhaps her most poignant self-evaluation is the one she makes, semi-inebriated, to Doctor Holcomb just before she departs her wedding: " 'I mean, not that someone should ever want to come home to stay, but that just to be understood for what you are, neither to be loved to death nor despised just because you're young.' " (*LDD*, 304) A few pages later, in her final outburst against Helen, she becomes still more analytical:

> "You're like all the rest of the sad neurotics everywhere who huddle over their misery and take their vile, mean little hatreds out on anybody they envy. You know, I suspect you've always hated me for one thing or another, but lately I've become a symbol to you you couldn't stand. . . . The terrible thing is that you hate yourself so much that you just don't hate men or Daddy but you hate everything, animal, vegetable, and mineral. Especially you hate me. Because I've become that symbol. I *know* I'm not perfect but I'm free and young and if I'm not happy I at least know that someday I *can* be happy if I work at it long enough. I'm free." (*LDD*, 311–12)

Or so she thinks and appears to be.

If Peyton has been enslaved by other Solitaries in their quests for the fulfillment of unrealized promises, she has been left as a result with no clear idea of what her own personal promises even are. She takes to drink and nymphomania, becomes financially irresponsible, forgetful, lost, and finally suicidal. A telling moment in Peyton's life comes immediately after she and Harry have escaped the disastrous wedding reception and await the ferry. Swigging hard on a whiskey bottle, she berates him for his "behavior" on that occasion. When he makes too fond a remark about another young woman with whom he had spoken, she sounds more than vaguely like her mother in these early moments of her own marriage: " 'Can't you keep your mind off these girls? Good *God*, Harry, on our wedding day! With all these other things happening, too. When I needed you. Do you think I'm just someone you can walk off and neglect and forget? You've done it before and you'll do it again, I know, and we're going to have a rotten, rotten time if you don't watch out.' " (*LDD*, 319) She is attempting to enslave Harry in her own vision just as she has been enslaved in Helen's and Milton's. Though she gets away with an ill-chosen verb in the lines just cited, she mischooses again when she says a moment later " 'I married you because I need you.' " (*LDD*, 319) To which Harry replies " 'Need?' " Peyton stumbles in her attempt to rectify her error, but Harry presses the issue and joins the two words that are perhaps the ultimate contradiction of the Styron universe when he says " 'Need? Love?' " (*LDD*, 320)

In the terms I have been employing, *Love* is a quality which is aligned with the ability to Transfer, the ability to perceive the universe from some other perspective than one's own Solitary vision; *Need* indicates the opposite of Transfer, the inclination to estimate another insofar as he or she fits the requirements of one's own exigencies and purviews. Later, Harry will tell Peyton that she has lost the ability to love, and this is probably the first indication he has of that. Her own Solitary vision is for the first time attempting to shape itself, now that she is free of the dual burdens of Helen and Milton; but it takes shape along the lines of the examples she has had. So, too, does the human race compound its eternal problem when each individual shapes his behavior in accord with the example of history. The lesson seems to be one of use or be used. Peyton has known what it is like to be used. Now she will attempt to take control for herself, much as such other ill-used Styron heroes have: Nat Turner killing the person he loves most to demonstrate his ability to control life; Sophie sacrificing Wanda—both in Warsaw and in her later calumnies to Stingo—in order to save her life first and her face later; and Captain Mannix force-marching his company to win the battle of egos with Colonel Templeton.

Much analysis has been afforded Peyton's soliloquy, and I don't think I need redo much of that here.[9] Suffice it to say that we see the collision of Love and Need—Transfer and Fortune-forcing— throughout that eloquent, if also highly imitative, passage. Tony the milkman serves certain emotional needs for Peyton, and he is willing to be so used in order to satisfy his own sexual urges upon her. This, of course, is not love; it is a sort of tacit mutual enslavement. From what we know of it, the affair with Earl Sanders of Darien must have been much the same. In terms of my present investigation, Peyton's soliloquy is more instructive in what it demonstrates about Guilt and Transfer, but I would like to look briefly at Dolly Bonner and Carey Carr before considering those matters.

Dolly Bonner and Carey Carr

> She had been much publicized for her social activities—Red Cross, the Women's Club, and the like—and her picture, taken shortly after her wedding, had been printed in the local papers sometimes as often as twice a month for over a period of twenty years until finally even she sensed the impropriety of the cloche hat and bangs which had given rise to idle and secret laughter around town. So she had had the picture replaced, regretfully, with another, newer one in which there no longer blossomed the youthful smile, but which instead recorded with precision the small puffy folds beneath her eyes and her neck, too, flaccid and slightly wrinkled. (*LDD*, 41)

In such description of Dolly Bonner, and later Carey Carr as well, Styron uses his subordinate characters to underscore his main themes. Here we have Dolly stoically yielding to the predictable, though nonetheless dreadful, ravages of Time and Fortune, though yielding all at once rather than gradually by waiting twenty years to replace her youthful picture. Dolly is not only pursuing the standard course of the Solitary in her affair with Milton Loftis, the attempt to force life onto an acceptable course; but also, like Peyton in her soliloquy, she is willing to be enslaved by another's *needs*, not *love*, in order to gain a measure of satisfaction and identity for herself.

When she and Milton first recognize each other's needs, Dolly tells Milton that she is not happy because her husband, Pookie, "'isn't a handsome man . . . he's a funnyman.'" (*LDD*, 61) Milton, apparently, is sufficiently handsome and unfunny—or, better stated, he is sufficiently different. The difficulties arise between them over this matter of enslavement to each other's visions: Dolly is willing, Milton is not. He yearns for a political career, so Dolly imagines herself a National Committeewoman in the confidence of Eleanor Roosevelt. In return she tacitly expects that he will service her own fantasies: "love, a marriage, maybe, in New Orleans, the Skyline Drive." (*LDD*, 74) Milton is not cut of this cloth, however, for Dolly is little better than a sexual release after traumatic showdowns in the Loftis parlor or mere company when he has virtually no one else to whom he can turn to alleviate his solitariness. On the occasion of Peyton's funeral, and on *many* other occasions as well, he speaks continuously of Peyton when Dolly wants him to speak, if not continuously at least occasionally, of her. Rarely does this occur.

Dolly can compromise to find some degree of happiness, though I do not think this is the sort of compromise that Carey Carr (to the extent that he speaks for Styron) refers to as the sort Helen should have made. Dolly's compromise still has a heavy amount of Fortune-forcing about it, for it can accept only one eventuality as an acceptable result. If she is only mildly disappointed that her career as a Washington socialite never materialized, she is desperate that, even with divorce imminent, Milton will never be able to detach himself sufficiently from Helen and the memory of Peyton to marry her. "It was so sad—but no, he wouldn't leave her: then he'd have no one, no Helen, no Peyton, no little Maudie, no Dolly-pooh. Which was what he'd called her when, nights at the club, they lay awake all tired out and watched the ivy shake against the moonlight and she'd stick her finger, playfully, in his navel. Almost two years of bliss, free of that ghostly bitch. Now this." (*LDD*, 323) This is the promise and realization theme once again. But, rather than being adaptable, Dolly becomes a fatalist: "She'd have to leave town, go to Norfolk or Richmond, or back to Emporia and sit by her mother's bedside, watch the withered, wasting flesh of multiple sclerosis, look at her twitch and moan, change her clothes when her sphincter gave way. . . ." (*LDD*, 323–24)

Carey Carr, on the other hand, is a man for whom the progressive realization of earthly promises augurs no respite from the spiritual promises which seem, apparently, unrealizable. An effeminate man, he had "in general cast out his womanish failings" (*LDD*, 107) by young adulthood, married, and begun climbing the "high slopes" (*LDD*, 106) where God dwelt, presumably so he would not die "tricked and cheated" (*LDD*, 107) by life as his mother claimed on her deathbed to have been. Throughout his relationship with Helen, however, he is victimized by "the strange and tragic sorrow he felt at never having been able to attain a complete vision of God." (*LDD*, 107) Though he can tell the distraught Helen that God "gives His greatest reward to those whose fight is desperate and whose struggle at the bleakest hour seems most hopeless" (*LDD*, 127), he is in no way certain of that. He is intimidated by the irony that, although God has not revealed Himself to him, he "must make her see . . . must bring them together." (*LDD*, 143) Throughout the remainder of the novel, Carey Carr voices virtually every degree of agnosticism, atheism, and—at the moment of Milton's physical attack on Helen—spiritual despair: " 'Oh, my Lord, You never shall reveal Yourself!' " (*LDD*, 388)

Although he divides the experiences into two separate characters in *Lie Down in Darkness*, Styron is portraying in Helen and Carey the prototypical emotion which seems to underscore the tragic nature of his universe: the futile quest for the realization of material promises which yields to the subsequent search for an absent God to explain to the Solitary what the quest should have been directed toward from the start.

The Search for Emancipation

As we have seen in *Sophie's Choice* and *The Confessions of Nat Turner*, Styron regularly raises the question concerning God as to who left whom? Has God provided no guidance to man in this universe, or has man been so hardened by his quest for Fortune that he has become too insensitive to hear His message. In *Sophie's Choice*, final emphasis would imply the latter. Nat Turner suggests that about his own situation late in his story as well. The answers given in *Lie Down in Darkness* conform to the pattern.

As we have already seen here, and in the other novels, there is much loose talk about God among Styron characters. He can be an invisible stand-in to provide imaginary solace when the Solitary vision is on the rocks, or He can be a hidden whipping boy to take the blame for miscreating the universe. Or, to really retaliate against Him and put Him in his place, He can be denied existence. As in the other novels, the scenes must be studied in which characters are earnestly considering the matter of God, such as Stingo and Nat do in the late pages of their stories.

On the occasion of Milton telling Helen that " 'we have lost our lovewords' " that I discussed earlier, he adds a footnote which is instructive: " 'We have lost our lovewords . . . what are they now? "I am the Resurrection and the Life." What does that mean?' " (*LDD*, 186) In these words we get the novel's first criticism of those who mistake the accidentals and myths of religion for its life-giving and life-sustaining spirit—the stand-in God for a less-defined but much more real sense of God. In her soliloquy Peyton expresses her guilt over her treatment of Harry and recalls his statement about God which is much more to Styron's point: "God is life-force, love, whatever you will, but not death." (*LDD*, 340) (Luigi, the fascist policeman of Styron's second novel, uses similar words.) Peyton extends this some twenty pages later: "I beseech you, oh Lord, and make me clean and pure and without sin; God, give me my Harry back, then, Harry, give me my God back, for somewhere I've lost my way. . . . " (*LDD*, 359) Contrary to Helen's post-Maudie defiance, in which Milton *becomes* her God, and contrary to Carey Carr's god whom Helen calls a "silly ass" (*LDD*, 299), Peyton will find God in returning the love that Harry has tried to give her. But she has forsaken Harry and so has done the same to God: "oh my God, why have I forsaken You?" (*LDD*, 382) This message is constant in Styron: in forsaking the love of other human beings, the individual strips himself of the ability to find God; in this inability to find God one imprisons oneself in one's own Solitary vision, desperately attempts to actuate it, feels little if any guilt, and so creates evil. However, whether Styron is speaking of Sophie, or Nat, or Peyton as he is in the following quote, the course of history to this date in the tawdry record of the human race has simply provided little example of what proper human intercourse should be: "I thought, oh Christ, have mercy on your Peyton this evening not because she hasn't believed but because she. No one had a chance to. ever." (*LDD*, 384) Peyton, like many, has not "seen God" because she has never seen the proper course for finding Him demonstrated.

Throughout this study I have been insisting that man's inability to feel Guilt is the source of Evil, yet we hear much talk of guilt from Peyton, Milton, Helen, Sophie, and even some from Nat Turner on the final day of his life. Theirs is *ex post facto* guilt, however, guilt that occurs only after the evil is done. Often this guilt is better termed "disappointment" because the Fortune-forcing has failed, though in other cases it is earnest and self-accusatory regret, better termed "remorse." Nat's recollections of Margaret Whitehead's death might be a case in point. Often this guilt is misplaced: horrible as Sophie's choice was, she can hardly be "guilty" in a situation in which she was given no time to reflect and in which *both* children would have been exterminated if she had not designated one of them to be. Such guilt in Styron's universe is gratuitous, for it blinds man to the situations in which he *should* feel constructive guilt, and it makes guilt an after-the-fact consideration. Milton Loftis, for example, feels guilt that Maudie has been born as she has and that he has not loved her as much as Peyton. Yet he cannot feel the sort of anticipatory guilt that would have him in place at the hospital on Maudie's dying day rather than at a football game and a fraternity bacchanal.

In a very pertinent passage, Milton properly assesses his own impotence and misdirection on the matter of guilt: he has just kissed Dolly at Peyton's birthday party and knows that his affair with her is all but consummated. He also recognizes that Helen is in great distress over Maudie's condition: "He wanted to comfort her a little, but he couldn't bring himself to do it. If it weren't for that kiss, he thought, I'd be in the clear, in the right. Guiltless I could comfort her. She was so wrong. She was so wrong, yet right too. . . . The kiss he had sealed upon Dolly's lips had sealed up for him, also, the knowledge of guilt, and there didn't seem to be any way of going back at all." (*LDD*, 96) Milton's guilt deprives him of his moral sense because it comes too late; it is not the instructive emotion toward Transfer that it should be.

Are there any examples of Transfer in this novel? I think there are, though I would be reluctant to label them exactly that because the full formulation of the concept is still a quarter-century off in Styron's canon. The very real identification the waitress Hazel feels with Milton's distress on the day of Peyton's funeral smacks of it. So also does much of Carey Carr's loyal attendance of Helen despite the depths of her spiritual depravity. I think the strange relationship of Maudie with the "magic man" Bennie is something of the sort as well. Perhaps the most thematically stressed ones, however, are in Chapter Seven, in the section heavily dominated by Peyton's soliloquy.

Styron opens that chapter with a lengthy essay on Potter's Field in New York, "transferring" in that he attempts to return their humanity to those nameless souls entombed there, in that he asks the reader to image for himself what such an end implies for the meaning of his own existence, and in that he broadens the physical reality of Hart's Island to nearly "every great city in the world—islands in the Thames and Danube and the Seine, and in the yellow waters of the Tiber." (*LDD*, 326) This heightened and broadened awareness is the foundation stone for what I have been calling Transfer.

Shortly after this we are given a scene between Peyton and Harry which describes their meeting in terms very similar to those of Nathan's and Sophie's. She is in distress with a headache, he aids her, he tells her of her beauty. From this point on in the novel, Harry becomes, in terms of Transfer, the most admirable character in the story. He continually tries to rekindle his love after each of Peyton's affairs. His friends aid him in protecting her, and one even gets her psychiatric treatment much as Larry Landau got Sophie teeth. Harry is even ready to take Peyton back again toward the end of her final day, dismissing her only when she virtually accuses him of having no ability to Transfer: "'You've just never tried to see my side of the matter, have you?'" To which he rightly replies, "'Haven't tried, my eye! That's all I've spent two years doing. . . .'" (*LDD*, 379–80)

With the exception of Tony the milkman, who insists that Peyton have sex with him despite her wishes and physical condition, her final soliloquy is dominated by people inclined toward Transfer: the soldier who recognizes her distress in the bar; the druggist who gives her a painkiller and urges her to get medical help; the old woman who gives her Aspergum; the taxi driver who tries to be tolerant and is left at the curb without his money for his efforts. (Contrast this man to the taxi driver who curses Stingo's father, not because he was not paid but because the tip was too small.) All of the people just mentioned recognize distress and suffering in Peyton, attempt to alleviate it rather than profit by it or simply ignore it, and so refuse to create or intensify evil, whether it be human evil or the simple misworkings of Fortune.

Finally, I think Styron incorporates his Negro characters into this early exploration of the concept of Transfer. While I personally stand with those critics who find his final emphasis on the Negro religious rituals too imitative of *The Sound and the Fury*, I do not find the contrast of the simple black experience to be otherwise gratuitous. If the white search for God is too complex and misdirected and the Negro quest too simplistic, the Negro finds his God on a communal occasion which is the antithesis of the solitary searches of his white "betters." Ella even rounds up a stray child named Doris to participate in their baptism with them and so protect the child till her parents turn up. I would like, however, to cite another instance of Negro participation in the plot to demonstrate what Styron understands to be their racial instinct to Transfer.

Near the end of Chapter Four La Ruth goes upstairs to inform Helen that Carey Carr has arrived to take her to the cemetery. Helen, of course, feels nothing resembling the normal parental grief at the loss of a child, but La Ruth does not know this. Instead she stands aside admiring her mistress's "courage":

> La Ruth stood there motionless, with grasshopper eyes, touched with dim, blossoming wonder at this victim of tragedy who, not once but twice now bereft of motherhood, could suffer so stoically and wake up from a hot day's sleep like this without hysteria. She herself had lost two of her three children and although she couldn't rightly place the father of either of them she could recall with what fright she had awakened for many days afterward, shrieking, blubbering crazily for God to send down his Apostle. Quick. To lead her not into paths of Belief (because she believed, anyway, with every part of her soul and body) but into paths of peace and grace. . . . And soon God had not just sent his Apostle, but had come himself, in a Cadillac, to make sure that everything was all right no matter

how much she had worked and sinned, no matter the children she had lost: Daddy Faith, who was the King of Glory, Wonderful, Counsellor, the Mighty God, the Everlasting Father, the Prince of Peace. . . . Helen stirred, placed her feet shakily on the floor and looked up once more into La Ruth's stricken face that pleaded for understanding—that tried to tell her that she, Helen, too, was qualified for the million . . . blessings, blessings flowing free for all that slaved and sweated and were acquainted with grief, or had ever just lost a darling baby child. "Po' miss Helen," she said. (*LDD,* 144–45)

What La Ruth can do, that none of the main characters in this novel can be bothered doing, is share the pain of the sufferer, realize that it is the nature of the world for all of us, color beside the point, and that, rather than in the castigation of God, the hope for the future is found in the "god" who emerges from the union of otherwise solitary individuals in a mutually sustaining community. If Daddy Faith is portrayed on one level as the worst sort of charlatan, he at least understands the human needs that make his charlatanism profitable. And this is far more than the white characters do.

While there is much merit to Maxwell Geismar's remark that, as in Salinger, Styron is saying that "this yearning for the experience of innocence may also be the attempt, neurotic or sentimental, to avoid facing the insuperable evils of the present,"[10] Styron seems to indicate that the instinct toward Transfer is a function of innocence as well. It is an innocence, however, that man has progressively and historically purged himself of in an ever-more-complex and ever-more-intense battle to impose his will upon blind Fortune. In the several Styron works we have so far examined, it is the young or the unworldly who speak the final message: the boys who cover Stingo on the beach, Margaret Whitehead, and, now, La Ruth and Ella Swan.

Somewhat the same response might be made to John O. Lyons who says that Styron is documenting the spiritual and emotional malaise of the Loftis family and "suggests that theirs is a universal situation, but the characters themselves see the predicament as unique to the time and place and so they look to some past time as a time of happiness."[11] In the present terms, the mistake is to return to the time of pure promise, before the realizations had a chance to be found wanting, and idealize that time at the expense of one's present self. However, the past is also the time before the forcing of Fortune was begun or even thought necessary. It was, in other words, a time when man's fundamental human goodness and "godliness" was available to him, before he found it necessary to create evil and, perhaps, detest himself for doing so. Jan B. Gordon calls this Styron's preference in his fiction for *nostalgia* over *memory*, for "nostalgia tends to screen those traumatic aspects of memory in favor of aestheticization which takes a segment of time and spatializes it. . . . Nostalgia is a collective experience—an attempt, often sentimental, by a civilization to write its own history."[12]

Obviously the overly-romantic aspects of *nostalgia* must be seen for what they are; but so also must the basic human instinct toward the purity and goodness of motive which typify those romantic visions be seen for what *it* is: the urge to live their lives, and live in life, some other way than the meretricious way most men, certainly not just the Loftises, go about doing it.

Notes

1. Forkner, p. 932.
2. Forkner, p. 933.
3. Ihab Hassan, *Radical Innocence: Studies in the Contemporary Novel* (Princeton, N.J.: Princeton University Press, 1961), p. 125.
4. Ratner, p. 36.
5. Ratner, p. 39.
6. *Lie Down in Darkness* (Indianapolis: The Bobbs-Merrill Company, Inc., 1951). All page numbers refer to this edition.
7. Ratner, p. 37.
8. Geismar, p. 249.
9. See especially Ratner, pp. 48–51.
10. Geismar, p. 246.
11. John O. Lyons, "On *Lie Down in Darkness*," in Morris and Malin, p. 95.
12. Jan B. Gordon, "Permutations of Death: A Reading of *Lie Down in Darkness*," in Morris and Malin, p. 105.

5

THE STRUGGLE OF
THE MANICHEES
Set This House on Fire

Set This House on Fire was a long time coming in a period when readers and critics had not gotten accustomed to just how long Styron would be in producing the awaited "next" novel. With the exception of *The Long March*, Styron went nine years between his first and second novels. Though it is often bombastic and definitely too long at 200,000 words, I cannot agree with critics like Richard Foster who says that it is "an orgy of commerce pure and simple. There is nothing good about it. Nothing true."[1] Nor can I support the over enthusiastic counterclaims of a critic so respected as Louis D. Rubin, Jr., who insists that, "despite a grievous structural flaw" it is an "even better novel" than *Lie Down in Darkness* which in itself was "remarkable."[2] There are memorable sections, worthy of Styron at his best: the destruction of the black sharecropper's humble shack by Cass Kinsolving and Lonnie; Cass's seduction of (or by) the *Watchtower* girl in Wilmington, North Carolina; Mason Flagg attempting to tell his mother that he has been kicked out of yet another school, this time for seducing the simple-minded daughter of an oyster fisherman in the church basement; the savage card game with the boorish McCabes. But there is also the terribly protracted analyzing of the fascist policeman Luigi, the overdone hunt scene in which Cass finally tracks Mason down, Cass's verbose attempts to tear down "the walls which had long shut in his recollection." (*SHF,* 433)[3] In Styron's thematic development, however, one's opinion of the novel itself notwithstanding, it holds an important place, for it confronts the dimension of man which yields Styron one of his major subjects and many of his underlying themes thereafter: mankind's ability to do great good and create great beauty on the one hand, his equivalent (perhaps greater) ability to spawn the filthiest evil on the other. In no book does Styron approach that question more directly and metaphysically (as opposed to historically or behaviorally) than he does in this one.

The Manichean Dualism

Styron is very insistent on this duality in human nature, but critics have not paid much attention to the means by which he represents it. They are plentiful. In the first pages the narrator, Peter Leverett, tells of having nightmares in which a prowler lurks outside his window ready to do him harm. When he calls his best friend to help him, he gets no answer, then realizes the face that is peering in at him is "the baleful, murderous face of that selfsame friend." (*SHF*, 6) Later he speaks of "a half-dream, half-fantasy" in which he takes a Polaroid picture of a friend only to find the face of an "unearthly monster" (*SHF*, 124) instead when the picture develops. The point becomes Cass Kinsolving's eventually when Leverett begins to see a "second Cass" who seemed "an indefinable weird displacement of himself, rather, as if he were his own twin brother." (*SHF*, 237) Cass says of his own dreams and the actions they inspire in him that they are "half out of the devil, half out of paradise." (*SHF*, 248) Frequently the two principles war within him, "Kinsolving pitted against Kinsolving, what a dreary battle!" (*SHF*, 250) According to his diary he is afraid to look in the mirror "for fear of seeing some face there that I have never seen before." (*SHF*, 361) In reverse, Saverio, Francesca's killer, earlier spends much effort in convincing Cass to hire her so she can support her family. Throughout the novel, however, Styron seems to insist that, in man's dual nature, the evil principle is the stronger unless it is actively controlled. As Cass tells his diary, "I suspect that whosoever it is that rises in a dream with a look on his face of eternal damnation is just ones own self, wearing a mask, and thats the fact of the matter." (*SHF*, 364)

The character who most clearly represents the evil side of human nature in control is, of course, Mason Flagg, although even Cass who hates him and has killed him admits that he was *not* essentially evil—"just scum." (*SHF,* 249) "Scum" would seem to be defined as the person who makes no, or little, attempt to harness the evil within himself. In a sense, then, Mason has strong appeal to the baser nature of all human beings. Even Peter Leverett, whom Marc Ratner accurately calls "a fixed set of mediocre, bourgeois, and sentimental responses,"[4] feels Mason is "more imaginative, more intelligent than I, and at the same time more corrupt. . . . He kept me hugely entertained [and] yet permitted me, in the ease of my humdrum and shallow rectitude, to feel luckier than Mason—duller but luckier, and sometimes superior." (*SHF,* 136) Mason, contrary to Peter, has had no parental guidance—"[his father] always seemed oddly removed from Mason" (*SHF,* 76)—and when he gets into trouble, as he does with the oyster fisherman's daughter, his father buys him off. His mother, "Wendy-dear," indulges his youthful pranks, feeds him alcohol, shares the caresses with him she does not receive from nor give to her husband. His wallet is always bulging, and he believes that money can buy him pleasure (which it can), friends (which it can, if the definition is sufficiently loose), and self-assurance (which it cannot). Robert Phillips calls him "a debasement of the American dream,"[5] and most critics go along with that judgment. "A self-gratifying child who is completely insensitive to others,"[6] he is antihumanistic, anti-intellectual, even anti-beauty and anti-art.

Yet in all his self-indulgent evil, he is also insecure. There is always the other dimension still glimmering within him, the force of good which does not respect, indeed attempts to reject, the force of evil. We see him in a New York bar attempting to win friends by dispensing money indiscriminately. When Peter calls him a liar on the occasion of his own departure for Europe, "his face went pale . . . he raised his hands, fingers outstretched placatingly toward me." (*SHF,* 171) Though he momentarily protests, suddenly he is forcing a wad of French money into Leverett's hand, in the "sorriest act of loneliness, of naked longing, I think I have ever known." (*SHF,* 173) His parting gesture "was one of recompense and hire, and laden with the anguish of friendlessness." (*SHF,* 173) Later, when we see him praising Cass's shabby art, having mistaken Cass for the better painter Waldo Kasz, we see him craving acceptance by someone he considers "higher" in an endeavor the world at least considers meaningful. Mason cannot be alone with himself, for his dominant self is too horrible for even him to consider.

And so he attempts to dominate others. For Mason domination means two things. First, there is the sort of domination he practices on the homosexuals in the New York bar, the movie crew in Sambuco, and others whose acceptance he requires to assure himself of his integrity despite what his glimmering better nature tells him about himself. Second, there is the domination which allows him to wrest all the materialistic and sexual pleasure the world has to offer, the dominance of Francesca, of Peter, of his mother, and ultimately of Cass whom he reduces to a clown for his own idle amusement. This is the Promise-Realization theme again. American life in the twentieth century promises such success and pleasure, and Mason will have it, at the expense of poor people, at the expense of dipsomaniacs, and at the expense of the U.S. Army, Italy, and general human decency. He in short is creating the sort of evil Styron is so much more precise about in *Sophie's Choice.* And if the question of moral responsibility is ever raised, Mason has a battery of canned answers. He and his New York crowd are rebelling "'against the H-Bomb. A world they never made, . . . the legacy that's been left us'." (*SHF,* 158) When Peter accuses him of being a fake and a liar, he asks why Peter "can't make the subtle distinction between a lie—between an out-and-out third rate lie meant maliciously—between that, and a jazzy kind of bullshit extravaganza like the one I was telling you, meant with no malice at all, but only with the intent to edify and entertain." (*SHF,* 172) This is a distinction that no longer really means anything to Mason or, as Styron shows us here and elsewhere, to mankind in general. "Edify and entertain" have become such goals that the possibility of maliciousness is simply overlooked.

Set against him is Cass Kinsolving, an alter ego that troubles him in several ways. First there is the embarrassment of their first meeting when the tasteless Flagg, thinking Cass to be Kasz, praises Cass's worthless drawings for their " 'space [and] incredible humanity' " when Cass himself knows " 'there wasn't no more space and humanity in those drawings than you could stuff up the back end of a flea.' " (*SHF,* 386) Caught in his faux pas, Mason must rectify the situation by degrading Cass, something he manages to do primarily with liquor and secondarily with Cass's need for medicine that Flagg can obtain through the Naples PX. Yet even as he reduces Cass from drunk to tarbaby to animal, he knows that Cass is conscious of what is happening to him, that Cass is in fact "using" him for his own purposes, most centrally the curing of Michele. No matter how low he brings Cass, he never feels he has him absolutely in his grip. Indeed, Cass's own theory of Mason's rape of Francesca is that "he was raping me." (*SHF,* 443) In taking Francesca he was taking that which Cass considered most beautiful in life and that which had freed him, through his attentions to her father, " 'to come into that knowledge of selflessness Cass had thirsted for like a dying man.' " (*SHF,* 443) In Cass's statement lies another way in which Cass troubles Mason: the search for selflessness that contrasts so sharply to his own search for self-gratification. If bland Peter Leverett can be intrigued with Mason's ability to do evil, surely— if human nature is as dualistic as Styron suggests it is—Mason can be unwillingly intrigued by Cass's attempts to shed his own evil self.

Cass Kinsolving has been called a Kierkegaardian man of despair,[7] and this is a very helpful label. He realizes, in Kierkegaard's terms, the antithesis between temporal existence and eternal truth, between the decay and degradation of the world around him and the pure beauty of what it could have been had man behaved differently than he has. Even in his own life, embedded as it is in history which is headed downhill, he still holds out the hope of being what he could have been. On its most central level, *Set This House on Fire* is a portrayal of Cass's attempts to become what he could be, this set in stark contrast to Mason Flagg who does not bother and is willing to travel the irrevocable course of historical decay.

In his dissatisfaction with himself Cass seems to center on one incident from his youth which both exposes to him the evil that lurks within him (and, he discovers, within everyone) and establishes the post-facto guilt that impedes his self-understanding later on. This concerns the occasion on which he and the red-necked shopkeeper named Lonnie travel to a Negro cabin to "dispossess" the man of a radio upon which payments had fallen into arrears. Unable at first to locate the radio in the vacant cabin and then to find it cracked when he does, Lonnie flies into a rage and wrecks the place down to its most personal and pathetic knicknacks. He convinces Cass to assist him, and together they tear out the man's stove and turn it over "until [we] turned that poor little house into what looked like something hit by a tornado." (*SHF*, 378) Even on the scene Cass is "sickened to his entrails in a way he had never been, his newborn manhood—brought to its first test—had failed him." (*SHF*, 377) This is what Cass must live down but has been unable to by the time he arrives in Sambuco.

I have made much throughout this study of the concept of Guilt in Styron's universe, that mankind needs to learn it in order to cease participation in the Fortune-forcing paradigm of human behavior. Cass, as Luigi frequently points out to him, wallows, perhaps even luxuriates, in guilt. Yet so did Milton Loftis and so will Nathan Landau, characters far from what Styron would offer as models of proper human behavior. Again, I think the distinction needs to be made between what the characters refer to as "guilt"—which is more disappointment in themselves for not having made things turn out better or, perhaps, more in accord with realized promises—and what I think Styron would think of as "Guilt" in the constructive sense— the ability to foresee the consequences of one's actions if possible, the constructive vow not to repeat them if not. The first sort of guilt, the one in which Cass wallows through most of the novel, can produce yet more blind Fortune-forcing in the name of some murky higher principle: art, self-realization, freedom, whatever. The second sort will produce a heightened awareness of others and escape from solitariness into Transfer. The difference between the two is crystallized in Cass's reaction on the one hand to Poppy and his noisy brood whom he blames for stifling his creativity rather than have to blame himself, and his attentions to Michele and Francesca on the other which approach the level of Transfer. When he first enters Michele's poor home, his associative memory connects the place with Crawfoot's cabin: "The same thing, by God. It is the smell of a black sharecropper's cabin in Sussex County, Virginia. It's the bleeding stink of wretchedness." (*SHF*, 416) Through his attentions to Michele and his family, Cass futilely attempts to undo what he did to Crawfoot and to purge his soul of the evil he knows is within it simply because he is a member of the human race.

To a certain extent Cass sees the "right" earlier in his story than Styron's other heroes do in theirs. This, however, does not redeem a man such as Cass, for his own ability to rectify things, despite his vision, is not great enough for him. Where Mason can shrug off his duty to the less fortunate ("'you know as well as I do that if each individual American went around nursing every sick distressed Italian that came along he'd go broke in about a week even if he had twenty million dollars'" [*SHF*, 420]) Cass goes to the other extreme of self-loathing. His only relief, finally, is drink, one of the lies that Styron characters are often guilty of, probably the most prevalent. In his dipsomania, however, he sees himself to be aligning with his detested fellow countrymen: "'They have to drink because drink drowns their guilt over having more money than anyone in the world'." (*SHF*, 345) And even after understanding that human evil begins with the misuse of the less fortunate by "Fortune's Darlings," he knows, at least subconsciously, that he can only support himself by aligning with the American capitalism he detests. Not only must he cultivate his "friendship" with Mason Flagg for medicine (and less admirably for booze), but also even before he meets Mason he has to feed, clothe, and shelter his family with the proceeds from Poppy's American real estate holdings. He is "sick with a paralysis of the soul" (*SHF*, 269) when he is conscious of his own hypocritical and paradoxical existence, "an emotional eunuch" when he tries to put it out of his mind. In either case, his art winds up lacking fire and passion and, as a consequence, quality and integrity.

The Search for Salvation

There is some critical debate as to whether Cass is "saved" at the end of the novel. Richard Pearce argues that although "many critics conclude that Cass is finding himself as an artist at the end, . . . it is important to remember that he is escaping from the modern world and from his complex responsibilities to it. . . . Cass cannot choose being because being is dominated by the power of wanton irresponsibility, and because it will yield no harmony or connection."[8] David Galloway, on the other hand, says that Cass "through his very fall is to realize the meaning of life, and through Luigi's intervention he will be given the chance to live it."[9] I personally tend to agree, if not totally, with Galloway and others who argue for Cass's redemption.

I find such interpretations more in keeping with the view of the world Styron's fiction as a whole has gone on to develop. *Sophie's Choice* demonstrates that it is not blind historical force which is responsible for universal evil but rather individual acquiescence to the Fortune-forcing paradigm. Not until each individual, or at least most, separates himself from that historical pattern can the situation be rectified. Surely just because young Stingo has a vision of potential human goodness at the end of his story, we are not meant to believe that the human race will fall into step behind him. We know it did not. Rather we are given the sense of a curable ill, the answer to the question that Cass Kinsolving asks Peter Leverett: "'this business about evil—what it is, where it is, whether it's a reality, or just a figment of the mind. Whether it's a sickness like cancer, something that can be cut out and destroyed, with maybe some head doctor acting as the surgeon, or whether it's something you can't cure at all, but have to stomp on like you would a flea carrying bubonic plague, getting rid of the disease and the carrier all at once.'" (*SHF*, 128–29) Styron's answer, I think, is the former, and this is what Cass learns because Luigi, for all his tedious verbosity, teaches it to him.

Like Cass (and apparently like Styron himself),[10] Luigi had to purge his own soul of baser instincts. He still refers to himself as a fascist, and he can still claim that most Italian peasants are so "'mentally defective'" that "'they should all be exterminated'." (*SHF*, 330) But it is Cass's generous feelings and actions toward them that eventually attract Luigi to him—and convince him to let Cass escape a murder charge. If early in the novel Leverett's father is employed to focus on the evil man is capable of,[11] Luigi is the vehicle through which the solutions to this evil are articulated.

Other critics have noted Lawrentian overtones in many of Luigi's statements, such as this one: ". . . the primary moral sin is self destruction—the wish for death which you so painfully and obviously manifest. I excluded madness, of course. The single good is respect for the force of life." (*SHF*, 195) Cass, however, by his own admission hates the Life Force "that caused me to produce such a useless, snotty-nosed, colicky tribe." (*SHF*, 255) Luigi's instruction to Cass is that through his guilt he is sinning against the Life Force which, representing the positive side of the human dualism, compels man toward good, toward preservation of the species, toward the "birthright . . . to try to free people into the condition of love" (*SHF*, 362) that the psychiatrist Slotkin earlier spoke of. In other words his guilt has blocked his ability to feel good about himself and to convey the resultant love for others into exemplary activity which is diametrically opposed to the Fortune-forcing paradigm. It has made Cass into a man who emerges from his drunken stupor only long enough to sneak medicine to Michele (to assuage his guilt over the wrong he did to Crawfoot) rather than a man whose life exemplifies the positive side of the dualism. In this way he resembles Sophie whose blind anti-Semitism has evaporated into informed helplessness on the rail platform at Auschwitz.

I stand, then, with the critics who see hope for Cass's future, even though he does not become a particularly active participant against the evils he has despised throughout the novel. He is at least in the process of understanding what Luigi was trying to tell him at the very moment he removed his manacles and allowed him to walk away a free man despite the fact he was a murderer:

> "Simply consider your guilt itself—your other guilt, the abominable guilt you have carried with you so long, this sinful guilt which has made you a drunkard, and caused you to wallow in your self-pity, and made you fail in your art. Consider this guilt which has poisoned you to your roots. Ask what it was. Ask yourself whether it is not better to go free now, if only so that you may be able to

strike down this other guilt of yours and learn to enjoy whatever there is left in life to enjoy . . . . Consider the *good* in yourself! Consider hope! Consider joy!" Then he stopped. "That is all I have to say. Now I am going to strike off that manacle." And he struck it off. . . . (*SHF*, 499)

In Styron, as I have argued, the good man is the one who finds the good in himself and develops it toward Transfer, the ultimate manifestation of goodness. He is *not* the activist who attempts to correct evil with one stroke as Nat Turner or perhaps Sophie's father imagines himself doing.

In a sense the crime for which Cass could have been executed is the same sort of misdirected "goodness." He assigns Mason Flagg the symbolic value of all Evil in the universe and primitively stalks him until he can split his skull open and hurl him into the void. The entire episode is replete with animal imagery—he and Mason, for example, glower at each other when Mason is under his bed, "like a hound dog in a quizzical encounter with a trapped coon, . . . [Cass's] nose inches from the floor." (*SHF*, 460) Later the imagery becomes Neanderthal: Cass "rose, with a stone in his hand, and Mason rose with a knobby club, pale, to confront him." (*SHF*, 464) As Cass pummels him with the stone, Mason murmurs "Dollbaby" to him twice "in a child's voice," and Cass, at the word, halts and looks down to "see that the pale dead face, which was so soft and boyish, and in death as in life so tormented, might be the face of almost anything, but was not the face of a killer." (*SHF*, 464–65) Cass thinks *Children! My Christ! All of us!* He gathers up Mason's body and keeps it "for a moment close to his breast" (*SHF*, 465) before he throws it over the cliff. I see a clear parallel here to the murder of Margaret Whitehead and to Von Neimand's terrible moment at Auschwitz—the recognition of or at least the craving for human love and unity through an understanding of the common human predicament. "All of us," as Cass says, are trapped in an existence which has not relinquished what it has promised and so has frustrated us and caused us to behave as most of us, in calmer moments, cannot imagine ourselves behaving.

Even so innocuous a character as Peter Leverett must learn this lesson, and for him (and perhaps for the rest of us) it is learned through the clash of individuals mightier than he, the clash of the passionate and tortured Cass Kinsolving who is nearly suicidal in his quest for the good and the self-aggrandizing Mason Flagg who is equally energetic in his pursuit of Evil.

I will argue elsewhere in this study that Peter Leverett's narrative level is lagniappe,[12] though Styron's purpose for it, however gratuitous, is clear. Peter is representative of the person to whom nothing much out of the ordinary will ever occur, whose "vision is distorted . . . by his own inadequacy and mediocrity,"[13] as Marc Ratner phrases it. Hence, he is symbolic of the billions of human beings who will carry human misdirection into the mainstream of civilization and so secure its place there. No Hitler or MacArthur or even Bilbo, he is the sort that such as they, for Styron, can feed upon—unless something occurs which can make him ask the questions about life that most men fail to ask. His two days in Sambuco have haunted Peter with nightmares and unanswered questions, so he travels to South Carolina to visit Cass and, with him, root through their mutual memories of those two days to determine what the experience actually *meant* then and now *means* for the future.[14]

Stated in the terms I have been using throughout, Leverett must be rescued from his role as Solitary, lest he unwittingly participate in the creation of historical evil. In the first chapter we are given several hints as to exactly how self-oriented he is. On his last night in Rome he drinks in a cafe, his mood "dangerously close to self-pity" and feeling like "someone sitting amid the bunting and splendor of his own farewell party, at which nobody at all turned up." (*SHF*, 24) As he drives southward to visit Flagg, he "began to feel strictly alone, and except for the noise of the car to remind me otherwise, adrift in a boat, rudderless and without course on a black and starlit ocean." (*SHF*, 26) Even though he later makes inquiries into the condition of Luciano di Lieto after their collision on the highway and even pays his hospital bills for some years thereafter, Leverett's reaction at the time is entirely self-protective: " 'I couldn't *help* hitting him. It's not my fault'." (*SHF*, 31) Over and over he makes the same claim to various of Mason's troop and to Mason himself, although they are all wrapped up in their own solitary worlds and hence do not listen to a word he says. When Luciano's mother berates him for atrocities done to her home during the war, he shouts back at her " 'I'm sorry, lady! I'm sorry! I'm sorry! But I didn't bomb your house! I didn't bomb your house!' " (*SHF*, 35) Peter did not, of course, but his is the careless attitude of the Styron Solitary, as is that of Luciano's mother as she chastises him for her own sufferings while her accident-prone son lies bleeding on the roadway. It is the outlook which must be escaped. Not as solipsistic as Cass's, it is all the more dangerous for its ordinariness and banality.

Interestingly enough the first good man Leverett encounters in Sambuco is Cripps, the movie director. It is strange that Styron would place one of his clearest examples of Transfer in this novel at the head of a movie company which otherwise epitomizes the attitudes Styron is criticizing. Perhaps Cripps has learned through years of trying to make Solitaries perform as members of a group engaged in a common enterprise, but in any event it is he who tries to stop Mason's orgiastic behavior and maltreatment of Cass. " 'Don't you ever get enough, Mason?' " (*SHF*, 189) Simple as that question is, it explores the source of all evil in Styron's world—the blessings of Fortune, no matter how great, never are enough for most men. Another example of Cripps's ability to Transfer is in his conversation with Peter about the road accident. Not only does he consider the matter from Luciano's point of view as the injured party, but his further remarks about Peter's own suffering in the matter demonstrate an awareness of other men that Peter has yet to learn: " '. . . during the war, in Algeria, I was in a jeep that hit a child. It didn't kill the boy but it broke him all up. I know how you must feel. It makes you sick to your soul.' " (*SHF*, 109) In all, he recognizes a disease "especially among Americans. . . . A general wasting away of quality, a kind of sleazy common prostration of the human spirit' ." (*SHF*, 116)

This wasting of the human spirit becomes the counterpoint to the Greek tragic references that Styron makes through the novel. When Windgasser, the hotel-keeper, refers to the crimes in Sambuco as "overpowering twagedy . . . It's like the *Gweeks,* I tell you, but far worse!' " (*SHF*, 220), the reader cannot help but recognize his overestimation of the situation. Mason Flagg simply does not stack up as a tragic hero; nor does Cass, though Cass tries to. In line with Peter Leverett's father's statement that "what this great land of ours needs is something to happen to it. Something ferocious and tragic" (*SHF*, 15), Cass is trying to behave on a grander scale. He yearns to conceive of his life as meaning something in the universal scheme, whereas most of those around him seem to be quite content with having their lives mean something only in their *own* schemes, themselves incredibly petty. He reads and quotes from *Oedipus at Colonus*. He actively attempts to suffer so that suffering, as it did for Oedipus, might restore his goodness and make him heroic in a heroless age. Yet as David Galloway has pointed out,[15] Cass here is acting more like the earlier Oedipus than Oedipus at Colonus, for he continues to assume "the role of God," as Luigi would call it, until the final pages of the novel. God has allowed evil to run loose in this universe, in a Manichean sense has allowed it to gain more power than He has, and so Cass Kinsolving will set things straight. This is a version of Fortune-forcing that we have encountered on less noble levels before, but it is Fortune-forcing nonetheless and must be recognized as such. The significant difference is that Cass's actions, however wrong, are performed in the name of mankind rather than in the name of himself as most of Styron's other Fortune-forcers' are.

What Cass perceives himself to be doing is acting in ways that modern man, most especially a modern American, is incapable of acting. And the criticism of America, duplicated by both Cass and the Styronian narrative voice in Peter Leverett, is terribly harsh. Some critics verged on calling it unpatriotic when the book was first published. In later, more level-headed analyses, critics like Robert Phillips have pointed out that Styron's attack is not so much on America as it is on what "American public life does to man's private life."[16] Phillips has also pointed out that it is not only in this novel that the anti-Americanism appears but, perhaps more subtly, in the others as well—through the country club of *Lie Down in Darkness*, the officer's club of *The Long March* (and also of "Marriot the Marine"), and the plantation house of *The Confessions of Nat Turner*. In the present novel we get reference to the palatial mansion of Emilio Narduzzo of West Englewood, N.J., U.S.A., at both the beginning and the end, complete with a roadsign instructing passersby to "behold" it, despite the fact it has the architectural significance of a gasoline station. Americans throughout the story drive fast cars and motorcycles wrecklessly, shutterbug at quaint cultural leftovers they consider barbaric, and generally order the locals around. The dimwitted Saverio even clears paths through crowds by shouting out " 'Make way for the Americans.' " (*SHF*, 69) The movie company has appropriated the center of Sambuco for its own uses and ordered the populace aside. Tourists automatically refuse to pay the asked for price for anything, and this has taught the peasants to overprice their goods and practice other means of blackmail. The record as it is presented here is a bad one; and Cass runs ever farther southward in his attempts to escape his countrymen, of whom the appallingly banal, hypocritical, and stupid card-playing McCabes are typical.

Yet Styron seems to me to be more critical of the times than of America. It is simply that America is representative of the times. Perhaps America has "made" the times what they are, but such statements as this one, made by Luigi, suggest a wider view: " 'the vulgarity of our age is not confined to America, you see. It is a world phenomenon.' " (*SHF*, 344) The British couple Cass takes on in his first hours in Sambuco are no more admirable than the Americans who clutter Italy, nor are the numerous Italians who find devious ways to empty American pockets. If the impoverished Francesca has cut a hole in Mason's cornucopia by stealing from his house, many of her countrymen seem greedy pure and simple. And finally there is something poignant in Michele's understanding of America which reaches beneath the surface criticism Styron seems to intend. " 'Was it true [he asked] that even the poorest laborer had a car . . . and a stove, and a house with windows? Would it be possible, when he got well, and they all went to America together, to get Alessandro and Carla, and even the littlest one, a fine pair of shoes?' " (*SHF*, 213) Cass assures him that it is all true—and in a sense it *is* at least mostly true. It is what Americans have made of their beautiful dream *because they are human* that Styron bemoans. I think the novel is pregnant with the suggestion that Italians would have done quite the same thing had they rather than the Americans been favored by Fortune in the twentieth century. To quote Samuel

Gompers, those who have enough continue to live by a one-word motto: "More." It is anthropological, not national.

Richard Pearce calls the force which governs the world in Styron's second novel "wanton irresponsibility," and I suppose that is as good a term as any. It embodies all the components I have been suggesting—the Solitary, his guiltless duel with blind Fortune to realize life's promises, his failure to Transfer. Pearce calls the bestial Saverio and the hapless Luciano "the tragic and comic embodiments of wanton irresponsibility."[17] There is some merit to this as well, for it reminds us of the Darwinian and gratuitous nature of the Solitary's struggle for materialistic self-fulfillment. Neither Mason Flagg nor Emilio Narduzzo of West Englewood would like to admit that he was a less-than-fully evolved Saverio or Luciano, but I think Styron is suggesting that they, and most of us, are. Instead of holding such primal instincts in check, we have refined them and given them honorific names such as "free enterprise" and "the good life."

"Kinsolving," as Phillips has pointed out, is a name which suggests Styron's final thematic point. "Kin" connotes family, and Cass extends his love beyond the limits of his own family when he sees to the welfare of Michele's. "Solving" means the process of correction for a difficult problem; here the difficulties are those each individual faces in this life in trying to make it mean something. I do not wish to argue further whether or not Cass has found that by settling quietly down in Charleston, South Carolina, with Poppy and his children. Rather, the more important awareness of "kin-solving" is the Whitmanesque vision Cass experiences at the window of his Paris apartment.

In the most ordinary components of a Paris backstreet, Cass experiences a vision of beauty and harmony which virtually reveals God and the purpose of life to him. His description runs to 700 words, but portions of it are worth extracting because they pointedly suggest the concepts of time-relation and Transfer which I have been suggesting are the ultimate awareness of the Styron universe:

> ". . . I'll swear at the moment as I looked up it was as if I were gazing into the kingdom of heaven. I don't know quite how to

describe it—this *bone-breaking* moment of loveliness. I was almost sick with desire and yearning for what I saw. . . . It wasn't just the *scene,* you see—it was the sense, the bleeding *essence* of the thing. It was as if I had been given for an instant the capacity to understand not just beauty itself by its outward signs, but the other—the *else*ness in beauty, this continuity of beauty in the scheme of all life which triumphs even to the point of taking in sordidness and shabbiness and ugliness, which goes on and on and on, and of which this was only a moment, I guess, divinely crystallized. . . . And the strange thing was that it was in the midst of this, in the midst of a time when I was most wrapped up in self and squalor and meanness, I had a presentiment of selflessness: I mean, it was as if the crummy little street had been for an instant transformed into some grand, gay boulevard of my own spirit, where I no longer walked alone, but where so many countless generations of lovers and old women and dogs and children had walked, and where there would walk generations of lovers and old women and dogs and children yet unborn. . . . For a moment I was released from my own self, embracing all that was within the street and partaking of all that happened there in time gone by, and now, and time to come. And it filled me with the craziest sort of joy. . . ." (*SHF,* 256–57)

In many ways this is transcendental in the Whitmanesque sense, Lawrentian phallic consciousness, the life force of Dylan Thomas. For our purposes here, however, the literary allusions are of little significance. Rather we see one of Styron's clearest statements of the escape of the Solitary from himself into a pure situation of time-relation and Transfer. Cass will not be able to sustain it, and it will be long in returning to him. Other Styron characters will struggle for the same sort of awareness in other novels. In the long run, however, it is hard to imagine that, had he been equipped with such a vision, Mason Flagg could have been Mason Flagg as we know him, that American tourists could be American tourists as anyone who has traveled abroad knows them, that Nat Turner could have become the Nat Turner he became or slaveholders have been slaveholders in the first place. Helen Loftis could not have been the cold loveless woman she was, Stingo the sneering darling of Fortune he is at the opening of his tale, or Sophie the careless anti-Semite.

Turning finally to the villains of history Styron repeatedly calls forth, Bilbo could not have been Bilbo, Lt. Calley Lt. Calley,[18] MacArthur MacArthur, or—most of all—Hitler Hitler.[19]

Notes

1. Richard Foster, "An Orgy of Commerce: William Styron's *Set This House on Fire*," *Critique, 3*, (1960), p. 69.

2. Louis D. Rubin, Jr., "An Artist in Bonds," *Sewanee Review*, 64 (1961), p. 175.

3. *Set This House on Fire* (New York: Random House, 1960). All page numbers refer to this edition.

4. Ratner, p. 75.

5. Robert Phillips, "Mask and Symbol in *Set This House on Fire*," in Morris and Malin, p. 138.

6. Ratner, p. 78.

7. David D. Galloway, *The Absurd Hero in American Fiction: Updike, Styron, Bellow, Salinger*, Second Revised Edition (Austin: University of Texas Press, 1981), pp. 91–105.

8. Pearce, pp. 31–32.

9. Galloway, p. 96.

10. Cf. Chapter Three, n. 7.

11. See the discussion of Leverett's father in Chapter Six.

12. See the discussion of Styron's narrative form in Chapter Seven.

13. Ratner, p. 73.

14. See the discussion of Bergsonian time theories in Chapter Seven.

15. Galloway, pp. 99–100.

16. Phillips, p. 136.

17. Pearce, p. 31.

18. Styron's thoughts on Lt. Calley are included in *This Quiet Dust*, pp. 218–25.

19. For an interesting glimpse of William Styron involved in the composition process of *Set This House on Fire*, see Arthur D. Casciato, "Styron's False Start: The Discarded Opening for *Set This House on Fire*," *The Mississippi Quarterly*, 34 (1980–81), 37–50. Casciato gives Styron's original opening to the novel and discusses some of the apparent thinking behind the author's decision to scrap it.

6

STYRON'S FATHER-FIGURES:
The Root of All

Although Styron tells us, both in *Sophie's Choice* and in an essay entitled *"Lie Down in Darkness,"* that his inspiration to write his first novel came as the result of a letter he received from his father during the great blizzard of 1947—"telling me of the suicide of a young girl, my age, who had been the source of my earliest and most aching infatuation,"—the raw material of the book was derived elsewhere. In a December, 1982, interview in the *New York Times Book Review,* he mentions that his first novel "is a book which is really a mirror of the family life I myself put up with."[1] Helen Loftis was modeled on his stepmother, "as close to the wicked stepmother image as one can possibly imagine," and, to an extent, Milton Loftis was modeled on his own father.

Yet this is not the whole story either. In each of Styron's four novels we can see a more idealized father-figure who does not drink, does not do battle with a shrewish wife, does not flounder in self-pity and inertia. Most of these men are wifeless: Milton's father has lost his wife and now idealizes her; Alfred Leverett is apparently a widower as well, as is Stingo's father; Nat's father has fled to freedom (and so is wifeless) and his surrogate father, Sam Turner, seems quite independent of any adverse influence from his own. These seem to me more to represent the recollections Styron has of his own father who died in 1978 and to whose memory he dedicated *Sophie's Choice.* Because of his father's inability to control his stepmother, Styron for a time felt alienated from him "whom I really loved,"[2] and in his fiction he seems to attempt to repair his earlier attitudes.

This father-figure has crept into each of Styron's four novels in a very thematic role. While each is significantly different on the surface—the elder Loftis is muddled, Alfred Leverett bitter, Sam Turner idealistic, and Stingo's father wise—they are at bottom all built on the same model. Each has great affection and expectations for his son, each is moral and God-fearing, each is atuned to the decay of the modern world and the ambiguous glory of the past. Each is anxious to pass on his hard-learned worldly-wisdom to his son, both so the son will not have to learn it the hard way and so that he may carry a different standard into the future than his contemporaries have raised on their own poles. Styron's commencement address at Hampden-Sydney College in 1980 is a further celebration of these virtues in his own father and is reprinted in *This Quiet Dust* as "The James."[3]

It is the contention of this chapter that in one way or another each of the four father-figures lured the son on toward a future which was at least more humane and moral than the apparently preordained and destined one, whether or not this alternative were actually attainable. In doing so each is placed in sharp contrast to the "standard father" available to most young people of the materialistic, beautyless, amoral if not immoral age which Styron so frequently criticizes. Loftis's father, if ineffective, was superior to Loftis himself as a father and to other fathers in the book, such as Dick Cartwright's. Alfred Leverett did better by his son than Mason Flagg's father did. Sam Turner educated his black "son" and prepared him for freedom, an anomaly. Stingo's father cultivated his humanity, while Sophie's turned her into a bigot and passive advocate of genocide. In drawing such sharp contrast, Styron, as I argued in the discussion of *Sophie's Choice*, is placing the responsibility for the continued evolution of human evil squarely upon the shoulders of the progenitors of each new generation: do they continue to propel the promise/realization and Fortune-Forcing model into its irrevocable guiltlessness, or do they teach time-relation and Transfer? In the answer to such a basically simple question lies Styron's moral judgment.

The Elder Loftis

Milton Loftis' father comes equipped with the broad wisdom and measured loquaciousness of the other three and represents a dying ideal. *"I only trust you will heed the warning of one who has seen much water pass as it were beneath the bridge one to whom I must admit the temptations of the flesh have been potent and manifold, and that you will perhaps in some measure renounce a way of life which even in its most charitable concept can lead only to grief and possibly complete ruination."* (*LDD*, 14, italics Styron's) If Milton on occasion "hates" his father, it is because the old fellow's message seems built upon platitudes (*"keep your chin up and your kilts down and let the wind blow"* [*LDD*, 15, italics Styron's]), is invitingly ambiguous (*"Your first duty remember, son, is always to yourself"* [*LDD*, 15, italics Styron's]), and is overly optimistic and, Milton feels, wrong (*"Believe me, my boy, you have a good woman"* [*LDD*, 45, italics Styron's]). In retrospect Milton resents the fact that his father was too good to him, "lacked the foresight to avoid spoiling his son" (*LDD*, 15), and in general did not prepare him for the disillusionment his middle age would bring.

David Galloway, in *The Absurd Hero in American Fiction*, makes much of Styron's creation of absurd universes early in each novel.[4] The elder Loftis, perhaps more than any of the other father figures, is unable to recognize these absurdities or, at least, believes they can be effectively coped with. *"Most people . . . get on through life by a sophomoric fatalism. Only poets and thieves can exercise free will, and most of them die young."* (*LDD*, 97, italics Styron's) The paradoxes of modern existence are, to him, a challenge rather than an obstacle. For instance, when he discusses the ironic position of the modern Southerner who seeks to do right, that "right" seems much more available to him than it ever will to Milton: *". . . being a Southerner and a Virginian and of course a Democrat you will find yourself in the unique position of choosing between (a) those ideals implanted as right and proper in every man since Jesus Christ and no doubt before and especially in Virginians and (b) ideals inherent in you through a socioeconomic culture over which you have no power to prevail; consequently I strongly urge you my son to be a good Democrat but to be a good man too if you possibly can. . . ."(LDD*, 47–48, italics Styron's) The guidance for proper behavior is in the past not the future ("If the crazy sideroads start to beguile you, son, take at least a backward glance at Monticello" [*LDD*, 74]), but for Milton the past is irretrievable, the future inevitable, the present intolerable. His father's wisdom seems outdated, does not work.

To a great degree it surely evaporates for the reader trying to find moral consolation in it as well. Yet as always Styron allows the old boy to voice probably the most important thematic words of the story, and even Milton is haunted by their essential and undeniable truth. The following statement, despite the scatological metaphors, is perhaps the most central to Styron's theme: "we stand at the back door of glory. Now in this setting part of time we are only relics of vanquished grandeur more sweet than God himself might have imagined: we are the driblet turds of angels, not men but a race of toads, vile mutations who have lost our lovewords. . . ." (*LDD*, 184–5) At his deepest despair Milton recalls, once again, a line of his father's: "Ah, for a man to arise in me, that the man I am should cease to be." (*LDD*, 209)

However ineffective he is and unrealizable is his message, the elder Loftis stands as a memory of a better, more noble, more moral, more hopeful time. Milton is never fully convinced that the road back to that time is irrevocably blocked, nor I think is Styron. The lure persists, as it must if the human race is not to extinguish itself by the Schopenhauerian methods Luigi speaks of in Styron's next novel. However ludicrous his father's verbiage occasionally is, Milton knows that his father was a better man than he is, and the reader can contrast him to the more regular and "acceptable" fathers who populate the book. Helen's father, Blood and Jesus Peyton, sits confidently at the right hand of God: " ' "We must stand fast with the good. The Army of the Lord is on the march. We'll lick the Huns and the devil comes next. Your daddy knows what's right." ' "(*LDD*, 114) Or there is Dick Cartwright's who tries so hard to shape his son that he cuffs him overboard in thirty feet of water when the boy fails to handle the sailboat's mainsheet properly. Throughout his childhood Dick is torn between love and hate for him. He is occasionally surprised by moments of tenderness, but too often "there came foul weather . . .monsoon winds, smelling faintly of dollars, perilous transactions, heady enterprises to be sought on some distant hazardous shore." (*LDD*, 228)

The true father-figure in Styron is above all cautionary; the senior Peyton and Cartwright know no caution and proceed blindly into the future Styron fears, thereby creating it. They are men whose sense of Guilt is virtually undeveloped simply because they "know" what "right" is and, so, do it relentlessly.

Alfred Leverett

In none of his books is Styron more critical of America than he is in *Set This House on Fire*, and some of the most articulate and damning remarks he places, early on, in the mouth of Alfred Leverett, father of the narrator. Much more bitter than the elder Loftis, old Leverett (still alive in this novel where Loftis' father has long been dead) also seems to believe that the tide can be stemmed if someone—preferably his son—would be on with the stemming. During the visit Peter makes to see him in Port Warwick on his way to Cass's home in South Carolina, Alfred Leverett plays the full keyboard range of things which are bothering him (and clearly bothering Styron and perhaps Styron's father as well).

While they ride together through the "new" Port Warwick, father tells son that they are witnessing the "decline of the West" as they recognize that their once sleepy Southern city now resembles Perth Amboy, Bridgeport, or Yonkers. He inveighs against the " 'California influence' " [*SHF*, 11]) which will prevail in the end and will strip the nation of its leaves and greenery. Though not opposed to change *per se* (" 'Only fools lament change in itself' " [*SHF*, 11]), he objects to the "pillaging" that Americans perceive that change must amount to in modern times.

> "These are miserable times. . . . Empty times. Mediocre times. You can almost sniff the rot in the air. And what is more, they are going to get worse. Do you know that? Read Carlyle. Read Gibbon. Get times like these when men go whoring off after false gods, and the fourth or fifth best is best, and newness and slickness and thrills are all—and what do you come to at last? Moral and spiritual anarchy,

that's what. Then political anarchy. Then what? Dictatorship! We've
already *got one* in this state. . . ." (*SHF*, 12, italics Styron's)

Peter calls him "the only true liberal I think I have ever known"
(*SHF*, 13), carefully balancing "an honest piety" on one hand and
"enlarged human views" on the other. In short he is a man who
knows he does not fit in a world dominated by Mason Flagg,
Hollywood, Eisenhower, and fat cats who "can go to hell in a
Cadillac for all I care."(*SHF*, 14) In his ability to articulate his rage,
he escapes becoming what Cass Kinsolving became in Paris, Rome,
and Sambuco as he lashed out blindly at the milieu that stifles him.

In my discussion of the narrative structure of this novel I suggest,
counter to some critics,[5] that Peter Leverett does not belong as its
narrator and perhaps has no meaningful reason to even be in it.
Not so, however, his father, for Alfred Leverett keynotes the actions
that Cass will eventually perform: " 'What this country needs
. . . what this great land of ours needs is something to happen to
it. Something ferocious and tragic, like what happened to Jericho
or the cities of the plain—something terrible I mean, son, so that
when people have been through hellfire and the crucible, and have
suffered agony enough and grief, they'll be men again, human beings,
not a bunch of smug contented hogs rooting at the trough. Ciphers
without mind or soul or heart. Soap peddlers!' " (*SHF*, 15) In order
to find his mind and soul and heart, Cass Kinsolving puts himself
through hellfire both in lesser incidents with the dreary McCabes
and larger ones with the sated and evil-doing Mason Flagg.

When Peter listens to his father's words he feels, he says, "jaded
and depressed, . . . unaccountably weary and worn out—old before
my time—and I had a sudden sharp pang of total estrangment, as
if my identity had slipped away, leaving me without knowledge of
who I was or where I had been and where I was ever going." (*SHF*,
16) Yet his father touches him to the heart with his "old sweetness
and decency and rage, but also by whatever it was within me—
within life itself, it seemed so intense—that I knew to be irretrievably
lost." (*SHF*, 18) Once again, the father figure represents the lost
time which was, if not ideal, much better and which serves to spur
the son into dissatisfaction that he trusts will be constructive rather
than demoralizing.

And once again Styron peppers the book with the other sort of parent—Mason's, for example—who is indulgent, materialistic, image-driven, pleasure seeking. Mason's mother uses her son as a surrogate husband and reminder of past glory, and Mason is eager to respond by indulging himself in all the spoils glory seems to bring with it and require at the expense of other men—from a dim-witted local girl to Cass Kinsolving—less indulged and less glorified.

As in *Lie Down in Darkness*, the father-figure in this novel represents the opposite direction from the one in which "things" are going. In terms of Styron's thematic pattern as a whole, he represents a purer time before the great attempt to realize supposed "promises" through the forcing of Fortune began. Or, to use Alfred's own words for it, before he got around to "trading [his] soul for a sawbuck, and forswearing [God's] love." (*SHF*, 16)

Samuel Turner

Perhaps ironically Samuel Turner is a father-figure of the future, not of the past. The past is racist and slave-holding. Turner, if he is not ready to free his slaves or to believe that the Negro race is inferior only because of white repression, is in fact prepared to recognize the equality of at least one member of it. In so doing, he is ready to begin to emerge from the error of the past into the burgeoning possibilities for "right" in the future. If Turner is the only father-figure to look forward rather than backward, he is the only one of Styron's father-figures to live in the early nineteenth rather than the early twentieth century when things are beginning to collapse.

It is also ironic that forward-looking Sam Turner is also the only one of the four father-figures to create evil as a result of his words and actions. Not realizing that neither Nat nor the world may be ready for his own new awareness, he promises Nat something that he cannot eventually produce—he gives him "fanciful notions" (*NT*, 192) of freedom. Though the possibilities are initially so staggering to Nat that he tries to refuse the opportunity—" 'But I don't want to go to any Richmond!' " (*NT*, 194)—Nat begins to count on the realization of this promise, even on occasion brags about it to those less fortunate. But, not only does Turner's economic situation deteriorate before this can happen, he is also victimized by a "fetching ingenuousness and faith in human nature." (*NT*, 239) A poor judge of people, he retains belief in the inherent goodness of the clergy and chooses the Reverend Eppes to carry out his promise to Nat. Eppes has no intention of doing so, and Nat as a result comes to hate Samuel Turner in his memory. His promise unrealized, Nat plans his ill-fated rebellion. In Styron, it seems, the father-figure is always "out of sync" with the times because the times are always at odds with the moral law, God's plan, the natural law, or whatever one might prefer to call it.

What are we to make of Nat's actual father, long since gone by the time Nat is old enough to inquire about him? On the one hand he was apparently a man who had some awareness of his own human dignity despite the propensity of bondage to dispel him of any such idea. Like Nat he was "too smart fo' dat kind of low nigger work' " (*NT*, 133), and one day he simply walked off the plantation after his new master, Ben Turner, struck him in the mouth for insubordination. Local myth has it that he went to Pennsylvania to earn enough money to buy his wife and son out of slavery.

On the other hand that was quite a few years ago, and he has never come back. He was possibly captured or killed; but like Nat, he could simply have been seeing to his own needs, realizing his own promises. There are other women to have other sons by. Whatever Styron would have us infer, Nat's true father does not fit the role of father-figure that he uses so regularly in his fiction, most clearly in his failure to give his son guidance that is otherwise hard to come by.

Stingo's Father

We have already discussed Stingo's father to some extent in the consideration of *Sophie's Choice*. In terms of the father-figure type, this is the most fully developed one. If he does still have his trouble with a cab driver in New York—and so seems out of control in the age in which he has been doomed to live—this is surely just Styron's way, once again, of calling our attention to the fact that he represents something different and more admirable than we are otherwise likely to find in that age.

Where the elder Loftis and Alfred Leverett seem to spout random bits of occasional wisdom, Stingo's father more resembles Samuel Turner in that he seems to have a "program" for his son's development away from the apparent destiny of his peers. In the Hampden-Sydney address Styron humorously recounts his own father's attempts to find a college for him where he would not drink himself into a useless adulthood. Stingo's father does much the same by sending him to a "pleasant institution" to correct some defects that made him "difficult to handle after my mother died." (*SC*, 4) As the novel progresses, Stingo's father sends him "enough" but not too much to live on in New York. He keeps him up on the local news while Stingo labors in the North, "that no-good world" (*SC*, 448), and even triggers his imagination to produce his first novel by informing him of the death of Maria Hunt (the model, here at least, for Peyton Loftis). He even offers him Frank Hobbs's property as a place to write it and to research his lifelong interest in Nat Turner. Stingo at twenty-two may be an "adult," but his father has realized that he is still too young to be cast into a misdirected world, too likely to fall victim to the guiltless model I have been exploring.

In Chapter Two of *Sophie's Choice* Stingo delivers the encomium on his father that might best summarize both Styron's attitude toward his own father and, artistically, the role the father-figure plays in his four novels:

> I opened the letter from my father. I always looked forward to these letters, feeling fortunate to have this Southern Lord Chesterfield as an advisor, who so delighted me with his old-fashioned disquisitions on pride and avarice and ambition, bigotry, political skullduggery, venereal excess and other mortal sins and dangers. Sententious he might be, but never pompous, never preacherish in tone, and I relished both the letters' complexity of thought and feeling and their simple eloquence; whenever I finished one I was usually close to tears, or doubled over with laughter, and they almost always set me immediately to rereading passages in the Bible, from which my father had derived many of his prose cadences and much of his wisdom. (*SC*, 43)

Stingo's father teaches him the essential concept of Transfer, both in his reminders about people like Hobbs and Maria Hunt who have fallen before the world's onslaughts and through his own example. And this latter form of instruction has always been double-edged. We have both the punishment of his son for failure to Transfer—for the choice to cultivate solitariness—as in his abandonment of his sick mother to an unheated house, and his own continued attempts to stay close to his son in letters and in visits. "His motive was sweet and patently uncomplicated: he said he missed me and since he hadn't seen me in so long (I calculated it had been nine months or more) he wanted to reestablish, face to face, eyeball to eyeball, our mutual love and kinship." (*SC*, 188)

Sophie, on the other hand, had no such father: " 'I sometimes got to think that everything bad on earth, every evil that was ever invented had to do with my father.' " (*SC*, 466) Stingo on another occasion refers to her father as "a presence oppressive and stifling which polluted the very wellsprings of her childhood and youth" to the point that "she loathed him past all telling." (*SC*, 238) The evil his blindness and bigotry and hatred help to bring about will swallow not only those for whom he essentially cares little—Sophie would be one—but also those few mortals for whom he can truly feel love—Jan and Eva, for example: "It is impossible to speculate on the reaction of this tormented man had he survived to see Jan and Eva fall into that black pit which his imagination had fashioned for the Jews." (*SC*, 378) Because he lacks even the potential to feel sympathy for all men, and so to Transfer, he is able to sort out those whom he deems worthy to live and those to die. He assumes the role of God in his attempts to dominate the world of his solitary vision, loses his sense of guilt (if he ever had one), and so creates evil. This evil will destroy, almost mechanistically, his family, his nation, nearly the world, definitely himself. He is the grotesque combination of all the vices Styron portrays in the "regular" fathers—Helen Loftis', Dick Cartwrights's, Mason Flagg's—of the first three novels. And perhaps Colonel Templeton belongs on this list as well.

Stingo's father, on the other hand, is the master father-figure, the polished blend of all the virtues of his three predecessors. To the extent that he is Styron's own father, this is a fine tribute; to the extent that he is a fictional character he is an example of Styron's belief that the fine and good man can continue to thrive in the twentieth-century world, however rarely he seems to appear.

Notes

1. Michiko Kakutani, "William Styron on His Life and Work," *New York Times Book Review*, December 12, 1982. p. 26.
2. Kakutani, p. 26.
3. *This Quiet Dust*, pp. 279–82.
4. Galloway, pp. 81–128.
5. See Chapter Seven.

7

NARRATIVE STRUCTURE IN STYRON'S NOVELS

From *Lie Down in Darkness* through *Sophie's Choice*, Styron has narrated his novels in a way that is particularly consistent. Initially critics felt Faulknerian overtones—and surely those were present, as were Joycean ones—but he was never bound to them. Whether he narrates in the third person, as in his first novel (and in *The Long March*, though I do not think that novella fits the pattern I am about to discuss), or in the first person, as he does in his other three, the four works are assembled in essentially the same way. Before discussing tese matters, I would like to summarize the thoughts of two critics who have concentrated on Styron's narrative framework.

In an essay entitled "The Recollective Structure of *The Confessions of Nat Turner*,"[1] Ardner R. Cheshire points out some basic similarities among the first three novels. (The essay antedates *Sophie's Choice*.)

A man on his judgment day, reflecting on his moral responsibility for past actions and the possibility of redemption—this is an important motif not only in *The Confessions of Nat Turner* but in Styron's two other novels as well. At the beginning of *Lie Down in Darkness* (1951), for example, Milton Loftis awaits the coffin which holds the body of his beloved daughter Peyton. For the first time in his life, he must confront and assess the "evidence of all his errors." As he waits for Peyton's body to arrive on the train, Loftis returns in his mind to time past, hoping to find answers to the questions which have been pushing their way into the forefront of his consciousness: What did I do wrong? What is my responsibility in Peyton's death? Is there any hope that I can transcend my sorrow and my guilt? Similarly, in *Set This House on Fire* (1960), both the narrator, Peter Leverett, and the hero of the novel, Cass Kinsolving, are drawn back in memory to Sambuco, Italy, because of Peter's feelings of sorrow, regret, and recrimination, and to those old questions: *"What am I doing? Where am I going?"*[2]

If we were to attach Stingo's narrative to this, the questions would still be asked but would rather be formulated: "Given what I have seen and heard how should I act?" In other words, with Stingo a younger, greener narrator than the other three, he has the opportunity to not have to look back in regret or anger but rather to look forward with the information Milton, Cass, Mannix, Nat, and Sophie lacked when they made their critical mistakes.

Cheshire likens Styron's "recollective structure" to the philosophical theories of Gabriel Marcel, as set forth in *The Philosophy of Existence* (1949) and *The Mystery of Being* (1950), although he does not claim direct influence. At the center of Marcel's work is the distinction between primary and secondary reflection: "In primary reflection one views experience as a problem to be solved, as something which can be broken down and viewed objectively. In secondary reflection, on the other hand, one is involved in a very personal, sympathetic meditation of past experience."[3] According to Marcel, primary reflection dissolves the unity of experience which is put before it for the purposes of analysis; secondary reflection "reconquers that unity" in an understandable form. He refers to "secondary reflection" as "recollection," "the act whereby I recollect myself as a unity."[4]

The middle two sections of *The Confessions of Nat Turner*, then, exemplify the process of recollection so defined. According to Marcel, the occasion of recollection is never had until one feels an "ontological disorientation" which makes him unsure of the higher purposes and goals of his life, an occasion, therefore, in which he fears for his own self concept. He feels isolated and estranged from the plenitude of life which surrounds him and is therefore at cross-purposes with it. In Nat's case, as he sits chained in his cell on his judgment day, he has lost his God and doubts his own purposes. So he *recollects* in "Old Times Past: Visions, Dreams, Recollections" and in "Study War."

Cheshire goes on to argue that Nat has been victimized by misplaced fidelities and has as a consequence failed to achieve "ontological communion" with his fellow man. "Through recollection . . . Nat comes to understand why he feels such emptiness: he realizes that he has never entered into the redemptive fellowship of Being."[5] Therefore, the novel's final section, Cheshire feels, is a demonstration of Nat's entering "into a loving relationship with another human being:"[6] he moves from an "I-it" relationship to an "I-thou" one, first with the suffering Hark next door to him and second with the reincarnated Margaret Whitehead of his masturbatory fantasies. He has escaped "the voids of submission to authority and solipsism and achieved redemptive communion."[7] The terminology in Cheshire is more polysyllabic, but it seems to me not far off what Styron will come to call "time relation" in *Sophie's Choice* and what I have been more broadly referring to here as "Transfer"—the ability to escape the role of Solitary and experience existence both in communion with and, if necessary, in the place of other mortals.

While I do not disagree with Cheshire's analogy with Marcel, I would like to explore what seems to me to be the larger possibilities of another analogy, though like his it is based on little more than Cheshire's less-than-convincing foundation that Styron "has indicated his long-standing admiration of French literature and philosophy."[8] If one knows French literature, as surely Styron does, one knows Proust; and if one knows Proust he also knows, at least by indirection, Henri Bergson.

For me Bergson's analyses of the human memory and its relation to time are not so much at odds with Marcel's as they attack the problem from a different direction, one which authors such as Joyce, Woolf, Richardson, and, I suspect, Faulkner have found informative.[9] Bergson makes a distinction between the "Concrete Self" and the "Parasitic Self." The Concrete Self is the entire memory store of a given individual, all the experiences he has had (for Bergson none can be blotted from the memory) which instruct him about life and who he is as an individual within life. They tell him the places he prefers to be, the people he prefers to associate with or avoid, the activities in which he can most satisfyingly participate. These memories tell him, in short, who *he* is versus who someone else is and also versus who others would have him be for their own purposes. The Parasitic Self, on the other hand, is a channeling of one's memories into prefabricated categories. It is meeting a preset standard which either God or society supposedly demands. Conservativism or liberalism, Christianity or Judaism, self-assurance or reticence, all of these are preset standards in their own ways, for they repress the free workings of the concrete self and its full memory store by structuring the memories for pre-facto purposes which deprive individual men of their freedom to choose. Parasitic selves can be freely-embraced or they can be imposed from without: I can select Catholicism as a creed and abide by it strictly or, like Stephen Dedalus, I can be forced into conformance with Catholic doctrine for fear of the consequences. Also, parasitic selves can be consciously experienced, as in the two examples just mentioned, or they can be unconsciously experienced, as when a person, bitten in his youth by a stray mongrel, balks without knowing it at the very existence of all dogs.

When an individual begins to feel himself at odds with existence, his life seeming to move forward mechanistically rather than freely, Bergson says that person should examine the flexibility of his operative memories to determine whether they are being controlled by a parasitic self he does not approve of simply because it is at odds with experience as his suppressed concrete self understands it. Worded another way, he must consciously explore his memory store for useful and instructive analogies as to his true self, desires, and goals to restart the automatic memory processes (for Bergson the key to human freedom) which the parasitic self has shut down.

In Bergsonian psychology, the memory operates according to a schematic diagram, which is Bergson's own from *Matter and Memory*.[10] (See Figure 1.) Point 0 is the moment of encounter with a present experience, and Circle A is the body of immediate associations which the motor mechanism of the memory hurls forward to meet that experience. The child's association of pain with any

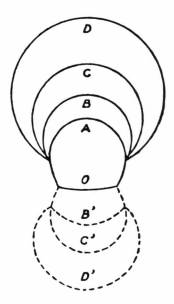

Figure 1. Bergson's memory diagram.

view of the stray dog who one time took a nip out of him is a basic
example, and Proust's tea leaves is a more literary one. The longer
one considers the present experience—say, perhaps, that it is a difficult choice of some sort—the more memories begin to come forth
to meet it; and these provide instruction in making the choice.
Hence, Circle B is the body of memories which begin to emerge
upon further reflection, and Circle B' is the instructive implications
of those memories: the child may begin to reflect on dogs who have
not bitten him and thus reconsider his fear. Circle C would be more
associative memories, C' more instruction: the only time *this* dog
ever bit him was the time he jabbed him in the ear with a screw-
driver. And so forth. It is in the free operation of this psychological
process that human freedom is found. The conscious or unconscious
adoption of a parasitic self, however, shuts the process down entirely
and predetermines the individual's responses to all present percep-
tions. (The reason there is no A' circle is that associations are
impulsive and become instructive only when the rest of the process
is activated.)

Where this all has bearing upon Styron is that Bergson insists that freedom is regained only by labored repair of the process, i.e., consciously forcing the circles to operate since they have been impeded from natural operation. As Styron's heroes reflect, they are forcing themselves into instructive memory groupings, and these groupings are called in psychological fiction, too simply, "flashbacks." I will attempt to demonstrate this in a moment, but I would like first to acknowledge another critic who has anticipated my point here.

Marvin Klotz, in an essay entitled "The Triumph over Time: Narrative Form in William Faulkner and William Styron,"[11] demonstrates that Faulkner was experimenting with devices of narration, mainly interior monologue, which he learned from Joyce, Woolf, and others. Styron on the other hand, with the notable exception of Peyton Loftis's 52-page interior monologue on the day of her suicide, generally rejects such experimentation and returns to a more standard chronological narrative in which, although a character is recollecting from a fixed present time, the flashbacks are more or less in a chronological order. Contrary to Faulkner, who pursues the apparently chaotic memories and associations of Benjy, Quentin, Shreve, the Bundrens, and others, "Styron . . . is above all a writer of powerful scenes which he is able to sustain at a high level of excitement for many pages."[12] His novels are "sequences of powerful scenes," particularly "those impossible social situations, 'scenes' they are called in colloquial parlance, in which one person or another refuses to abide by the standard conventions of behavior, and, as a consequence, a nubbin of embarrassment begins in the company and grows until it becomes so dominant and grotesque, the scene so tense and impossible as to create an unbearable tension."[13] Further characteristic of Styron's narrative structure is the fact that he also uses "delicate local flashbacks" which are embedded in the larger flashbacks. According to Klotz, Styron's main, perhaps only, rationale for ordering the flashbacks and the "sub-flashbacks" is their climactic impacts, although he still strives to maintain some chronological logic around them as well. Klotz, as others have, works out the general logic of the chronology of *Lie Down in Darkness* to demonstrate his point: Peyton *is* progressively older in the flashbacks of each successive chapter, though the lesser flashbacks which accompany each chapter do not abide as clearly by chronological rules.

In combining the arguments of Cheshire and Klotz with my further suggestions about Bergsonism, the central thing which can be said about Styron's narratives is that they are attempts to transcend the present "ontological disorientation" of the central characters by probing the full range of the memory (as opposed to the narrower dimensions of it by which they have been existing) in order to discover who they are, where they went wrong, and what it will require to untrack themselves and so regain their freedom to be who they were meant to be. Styron's dramatic power comes from his ability to order these climactically, to avoid the chronological confusion sometimes present in Faulknerian narration, and to have each set of flashbacks demonstrate an artistic unity.

Klotz's article confines its discussion to the first two novels only, and Cheshire centers on *Nat Turner*. With the arrival of *Sophie's Choice*, however, we can be more specific still about the favorite Styronian structure, both in regard to its components and its relation to his central themes. I would like to discuss these in order.

First, the full structure. A Styron novel operates always on at least four time levels, and once on a fifth as well. First there is what we might call the "Transcendent Present," the occasion on which the narrator sits back, puts his feet up, tells a tale. He is aware of himself *as* a tale-teller more than as a character in the story. It is, for example, the older Stingo who has done much research on the Holocaust and is now going to tell the reader a tale of himself before he had attained his present wisdom. It is Peter Leverett reflecting back on his relations with Cass Kinsolving, both in Sambuco and in South Carolina several years later. It is the voice in *Lie Down in Darkness* that tells the reader about the interior of railroad cars which no character has ever seen. It is the dream vision of Nat Turner as he awaits death in his cell. In short, it is a narrative voice not bound by the temporal or physical limitations of the main character in the story. It is wiser, older, transcendent, instructive. In Cheshire's terms it is the reconstructed self after the memories have been analyzed, in Bergson's the Concrete Self about to tell of its dark night of the soul under the domination of a Parasitic Self.

The second level of time in Styron is the "Narrative Present," the occasion upon which the flashbacks and recollections are sought and examined. The day of Peyton's funeral, Peter Leverett's trip to South Carolina to visit Cass, Nat's final days before execution, Stingo's summer in Brooklyn with Nathan and Sophie. In the first and third novels we have the main characters exploring their own ruptured personalities, in the second and fourth a naive listener trying to grasp the difficulties of a tortured second party. In all four it is examination of the memory in Marcelian or Bergsonian terms.

I personally prefer the Bergsonian analogy because of the literary possibilities of the Bergsonian diagram recreated in Figure 1. A Styron novel is active creation of the "circles" of memory; and the third level of time is roughly equatable with the upper (A, B, C, D . . .) circles, the fourth level with the lower, "primed" ones (B′ C′, D′ . . .).

The third level of Time, then, might be termed the level of "Major Flashback," the "powerful scenes" of Klotz's argument: Peyton's birthday party, her wedding, the day in Charlottesville; Mason Flagg's party in Sambuco; Nat leading the rebellion, or trying to; Sophie making her choice. These are the critical moments in the characters' lives where, if something went wrong, these occasions must have been material causes in themselves.[14]

The fourth level, finally, would be the "Embedded Flashback," those memories which spin off from the Major Flashback, usually (though not always) antedate that Major Flashback, and provide further context *for* the Major Flashback. Whereas in Styron the Major Flashback seems consciously sought out from the memory and then considered, the Embedded Flashback seems to be an unexpected associative memory which helps the character (and the reader) explain, interpret, and comprehend the full import of the Major Flashback. In Bergsonian terms, these are the primed circles which provide the instructive dimensions to our memories.

In one novel only, and then in only two places, do I detect a fifth level of time, a deeper flashback inserted into the Embedded Flashback. I speak of *Lie Down in Darkness*, and I will not try to say anything wise about those two unexpected exceptions. Perhaps they are of great importance, but I doubt it. Rather Styron was less sure

of his method in his first novel perhaps, or possibly I have misas-
signed them a stature they do not deserve. I do not consider, for
example, any undeveloped expository information as a time level
or a flashback—Farrell's brief reference to his son's death in Chapter
One of *Sophie's Choice* would be a case in point. Since the scene of
death was not portrayed, it is therefore "simple exposition" in the
schema I am suggesting.

I would like now to represent each novel fully in terms of its
structure, emphasizing the four time levels as they shift from one
to the other. I will begin again with *Sophie's Choice*, since I consider
it Styron's most perfect work in structure as well as in thematic
unity.[15]

Transcendent Present	Narrative Present	Major Flashback	Embedded Flashback
Chapter 1			
	3–10 Stingo working for McGraw-Hill reading manuscripts.		
	10–15 Stingo at home in the University Residence Club.		
	15–20 Fired by the Weasel for floating balloons out the window.		
	20–25 Conversation with Farrell about being a writer.		
Chapter 2			
	27 Stingo's "solitary banquet."		
			27–28 Visiting his grandmother's as a boy.
			28–29 Artiste's gold dollars.
		29	Father searching his mother's letters.
	29–33 Stingo reads his father's letter.		
	33–38 Stingo's arrival at Yetta Zimmerman's Pink Palace.		
	38–46 Meeting with Morris Fink and letter concerning Maria Hunt.		
	46–53 His first encounter with Sophie and Nathan.		
Chapter 3			
	55–62 Sophie and Nathan wake Stingo to go to the beach.		
	62–72 Argument with Nathan.		

Transcendent Present	Narrative Present	Major Flashback	Embedded Flashback
		72–73 The Bobby Weed Affair.	

73–77 Reconciliation and departure for the beach.

Chapter 4

79–87 General overview of Sophie's life and suicide attempt.

87–88 Sophie terminates her narrative with a statement of her "guilt."

88–106 Sophie's first months in New York: Blackstock, etc.

Chapter 5

107 Stingo receives his father's next letter.

107–9 The tale of Frank Hobbs in the letter.

109–19 Stingo's first attempts to write of Maria Hunt.

119–31 The meeting with Leslie Lapidus and two journal passages.

Chapter 6

133–34 Sophie and Stingo go on a picnic.

134 Nathan takes Sophie to Yetta's after library incident.

134–36 Picnic Scene, feeding the swan Tadeusz.

136–43 Nathan soothes Sophie at Yetta's.

143–44 Brief summary of Sophie's capture (Warsaw).

144 Nathan and Sophie listen to the rain.

144–46 Sophie's placement at Auschwitz.

146 Sophie falls asleep listening to *The Marriage of Figaro*.

146–47 Stingo recognizes that Sophie edits her stories.

147–48 Sophie sees picture of Höss at the gallows.

148–54 Biography of Rudolf Höss.

Chapter 7

155–56 Stingo and Sophie leave picnic, he to go to Leslie's.

156–57 Sophie's stay at hospital in New York.

157 Stingo comments on Sophie's and Nathan's "whirlwind encounter."

157–58 Nathan pays Sophie's bills; she "blooms."

158–72 Stingo goes to Leslie Lapidus's home.

Transcendent Present	Narrative Present	Major Flashback	Embedded Flashback

172–73 The meditation on Gide.

        173–79 The "seduction" of Leslie via Stingo's journal.

Chapter 8

        181–87 At the Maple Court where Nathan praises Stingo's manuscript.

        187–99 At the Maple Court as Stingo awaits his father.

        199–210 Nathan's attack on Sophie's morality and Stingo's heritage.

        210–13 Stingo speaks with Fink about the departure of Sophie and Nathan.

Chapter 9

215–19 Stingo's research, done in the 1970s, into the Holocaust.

        219 Reflections on Sophie as a victim.

        219–20 Sophie will tell Stingo secrets she cannot tell Nathan.

            220–33 Sophie's time as Höss's secretary.

                233–35 Höss learns that only Jews are to be exterminated.

235–36 Stingo's research into Richard L. Rubenstein's *The Cunning of History.*

            236–37 Sophie's arrival at Auschwitz concealing pamphlet.

        237 Sophie's admission of earlier lying.

            237–46 Sophie's upbringing, her hatred for her father.

246–48 Stingo's comparison of Poland to the American South.

            248–51 The execution of Sophie's father.

Chapter 10

            253–66 Sophie and the other cellar prisoners at Höss's.

            266–83 Sophie's attempts to seduce Höss.

        283–84 Sophie and Stingo at the Maple Court after her breakup with Nathan.

            284–87 Sophie's plea to Höss to see her son.

Transcendent Present	Narrative Present	Major Flashback	Embedded Flashback

Chapter 11

289–95 Stingo and his father after the fight with the cabbie.

295–98 Stingo's failure to stoke his mother's fire.

298–302 Stingo's dream of Sophie.

302–3 Sophie's scheme for Lebensborn.

303–9 Sophie gets drunk at Maple Court, prepares to leave Yetta's.

309–10 Allusion to the Connecticut trip.

310–14 Sophie reveals Nathan's drug habit.

314–17 The death of Blackstock's wife.

317–29 At Morty's party they learn of Göring's suicide.

329–31 Nathan suggests cyanide poisoning in Connecticut inn.

331 Nathan awakens her at Yetta's to go to Connecticut.

332–33 Sophie and Nathan in bed in Connecticut inn.

333–35 Speeding to Connecticut, Nathan calls her "Irma Griese."

335–36 In Connecticut bed, Sophie thinks of her mother.

336–37 The policeman stops them for speeding.

337–38 In Connecticut bed, Nathan dispatches the landlady.

338–39 Sophie performs fellatio on Nathan in Connecticut.

339–40 Nathan, in Connecticut bed, says he is drowning.

340–42 Nathan tries to urinate in Sophie's mouth.

342–45 In Connecticut bed, Sophie tells Nathan of her child.

Transcendent Present	Narrative Present	Major Flashback	Embedded Flashback
Chapter 12			
	347–54 Stingo and Sophie go to Jones Beach after his money is stolen.		
	354–56 Sophie tells Stingo of Jozef.		
		356–57 Jozef as a killer.	
	357–65 Sophie attempts to drown herself.		
		365–69 Sophie and Wanda captured in Warsaw roundup.	
			369–74 Wanda's plea for Sophie to aid them.
		374–77 Sophie awaits transportation to prison.	
377–79 Stingo's research on Birkenau.			
		379–80 Sketchy picture of the arrival at Auschwitz.	
Chapter 13			
		381–88 Sophie meets Dürrfeld in 1937.	
		388–400 Sophie, stealing radio, meets Emmi.	
		400–407 Dream of Dürrfeld and appearance at Haus Höss.	
	407–8 Sophie and Stingo late on Sunday at the Maple Court.		
		408–9 Sophie's suicide attempt in Swedish church.	
			409–13 Höss refuses Sophie access to Jan.
	413–14 Sophie and Nathan reunited at the Pink Palace.		
Chapter 14			
	415–22 Nathan loans Stingo money and they plan a trip south.		
	422–27 Larry Landau warns Stingo that Nathan is mad.		
	427–36 Stingo's visit to Jack Brown's; Mary Alice Grimball affair.		
	436–45 Stingo and Sophie flee Nathan after his threats on phone.		
Chapter 15			
	447–52 Stingo and Sophie on train to Washington.		
		452–53 Stingo, as a young boy, wins money on slot machine.	

Transcendent Present	Narrative Present	Major Flashback	Embedded Flashback
			453–56 Sophie disappears on the train.
		456–63 Sophie and Stingo register in D.C. hotel as the Entwistles.	
			463–64 Sophie's dream of Princess Czartoryska.
		464 Sophie and Stingo speak of their future together.	
			464–65 The dream is concluded.
		465–66 Sophie will now tell of her first day at Auschwitz.	
			466–75 Sophie and Wanda await capture in Warsaw.
			475–76 Wanda's prophecy of death.
			476–84 Sophie's arrival at Auschwitz; her "choice."
484–87 Stingo's latter-day reflections on Von Niemand.			

Chapter 16

Transcendent Present	Narrative Present	Major Flashback	Embedded Flashback
		489–93 Sophie and Stingo walk D.C. streets, get drunk.	
			493–94 The probable fate of Jan.
		494–95 Sophie says her heart has been turned to stone.	
		495–500 Sophie and Stingo in bed together.	
500–501 Later analysis of what next would happen.			
			501–8 The return to New York and discovery of the suicides.
		508–12 The funerals.	
512–14 Discussion of the three passages Stingo kept.			
			514–15 Stingo's night on Coney Island Beach.

Much more than in his other three novels, Styron has established a full-fledged plot in his Narrative Present; in the other books Nat is chained in his cell, Leverett and Kinsolving fish, and the Loftises drive from the train station to the cemetery. This is a significant departure for Styron from his earlier narratives; and it is related, I think, to the developing and more thoroughly articulated concept of Transfer. We must see Stingo thoroughly involved in the learning process, his despair, disillusionment, his eventual brightening of vision. It is Styron's portrait of the artist as a young man, learning the things which allow him to produce art. Furthermore, the Transcendent Present is *much* more thoroughly developed than in any of the other novels: the narrator in this time level has actually researched his topic and come to fully-articulated opinions about both his findings and the meaning of his 1947 experiences. This is in sharp contrast to the lyric reflections of Nat Turner's unconscious, the muddled curiosity of Peter Leverett, and the identityless Warren-imitator of his first novel.

Although less than he had done before, Styron tells his story heavily in the Major Flashback sections, secondarily in the Embedded Flashbacks. Now this is not to claim that *all* Major Flashbacks are equivalent to each other: they are not. It is simply to suggest that the Major Flashbacks are major only insofar as they are the punctures of the Narrative Present, the recollections which make that level of narration cease to operate and allow the story line to go in search of, Bergsonianly speaking, instructive memories. Once those memories are uncovered, they often invite attendant memories which give them context and allow them to act as instructive moments of past time. I say this not only in terms of Styronian narration; I say it also both in terms of Bergsonian theory and also in terms of human memory as each of us experiences it. Hence, there is no reason why the Embedded Flashback memory cannot be more dynamically meaningful (and consequently for Styron more climactic) than the Major Flashbacks which allow their Embedded Flashbacks to come into consciousness.

Let us explore just a couple of meaningful examples. In Chapter Twelve the hero and heroine go to Jones Beach for what is supposed to be a restful day's outing, especially in light of the fact, all psychological horror aside, that Stingo has also had his entire money supply swiped from his band-aid box. The Narrative Present leads not only to Jones Beach but also to Sophie's remembrances of the heroic Jozef and her real if temporary love for him. Her Major Flashback calls to her mind his heroism in contrast to her cowardice. Always suicidally inclined she makes her second-last attempt by plunging deep into the Atlantic Ocean before Stingo wakes to pull her out. Rescued, her next Major Flashback is to a similar example: the occasion on which she and the humanitarian Wanda were both rounded up for deportation to the concentration camps. At this point an Embedded Flashback, at least as important and dramatic, drops her back a short space of time to the occasions on which Wanda had pleaded for help, which only Sophie could have provided, to resist Nazi atrocities. In fear of being noticed and having her children subjected to further inhumanities, Sophie had refused, thus intensifying the guilt Sophie feels over the eventual consequences of both the atrocities and her cowardice, if that is the proper word for it. So her mind returns to the immediate result: the transportation to Auschwitz and, after a brief researched intercalation by Stingo, to the sketchiest recollection of the day she arrived there, surely the most cataclysmic day of her life. It will be three more long chapters, a hundred pages, before she can specify to Stingo, the first person she has ever told, exactly what happened there. This will be in a Major Flashback of Chapter Fifteen, perhaps the most important Major Flashback of the entire novel.

Another example of the shifting merits of Major Flashbacks and Embedded Flashbacks occurs in Chapter Six. At their picnic in Prospect Park Sophie tells Stingo three snippets of her earliest days with Nathan, these being the Major Flashbacks of that chapter. However, each leads her to an Embedded Flashback which is more ultimately important to her eventual outcome and certainly more dramatic than the larger flashbacks which embrace them. Also in that chapter, another Major Flashback is her encounter with the gallows picture of Rudolf Höss in a Major Flashback, but her real life experiences with him and the compromises she made (or tried to make) are placed in the Embedded Flashback. In short, the Major Flashbacks produce the memories which will help her assess, understand, and (at times) repair her present life; but the Embedded Flashbacks are the attached memories which grant those key recollections their actual significance.

Another dimension of the narrative pattern of *Sophie's Choice*, which we shall see to be in stark contrast to his first and even third novels, is the large variation in chapter structuring where there was much less variation in *Lie Down in Darkness* and less still in *Nat Turner*. Not only is Chapter One set entirely in the Narrative Present, but also so are Chapters Eight and Fourteen—early, middle, and late. These would seem to be, for Styron, those moments when the realities of immediately-experienced life force the memories to the rear, the occasions when life must be lived rather than analyzed: Stingo's youthful self-confidence which gets him (for lack of analysis) roundly canned; the crashing quarrel of Nathan and Sophie and of Nathan and Stingo which places all their futures in jeopardy; the occasion on which Stingo, off in pursuit of quick and immediate sexual fulfillment, accidently allows events to reach their peak and, eventually, bring about Nathan's and Sophie's suicides.

On another level, contrast these "Narrative Present" chapters to the ones which do the most continual shifting among the four time levels: Chapter Six which is Sophie's first elaborated revelation of the horror of the war years; Chapter Nine which is much more specific about those years and begins to expose Sophie's real guilt versus her better-termed "remorse" over what she was forced by Von Niemand to participate in on her first day at Auschwitz; Chapter Twelve which exposes Sophie's failure to try to act in time to prevent most of what we know eventually happened; and Chapter Thirteen which finally demonstrates Sophie at her most conniving, like Nat Turner a suffering victim out to take care of herself and her own at the expense of everyone else if need be. Note that these four chapters—six, nine, twelve, and thirteen—are the most complexly-structured in the novel; and they are those which delve most deeply and thoroughly back into the memory store. They are also the chapters which contribute most openly to the understanding of Sophie's own role in what happened in 1943.

Finally, observe the pure aesthetic variation Styron achieves here in contrast to the much more regularly-built chapters of his first novel. Chapter Eleven, for example, leaves the Narrative Present in favor of a heavily-orchestrated series of recollections of Sophie's and Nathan's weekend in Connecticut. The chapter begins to shift back and forth every second or third page between the chaotic drive up the Merritt Parkway in which Nathan tries to intensify Sophie's guilt for simply having survived Auschwitz when hundreds of thousands of Jews did not, to the scenes in the inn bedroom in which he holds the cyanide capsule between his teeth. Or there is the sixteenth chapter in which the Transcendent-Present Stingo creates an extreme tension between the devastated and Godforsaken young man who attends his best friends' funerals and the older, wiser narrator who, even though he has learned an alternative lesson about those days, must honor and honestly portray himself in a time when such vision was not available to him.

I would like now to parallel the narrative structure of *Lie Down in Darkness* to *Sophie's Choice* to demonstrate its much more regular, much less flexible pattern. Again, I would like to suggest that the only reason for this is not authorial inexperience alone. It is also because the concept of Transfer is much less fully articulated or experienced. Since Transfer greatly depends on Steiner's concept of "time-relation," the narrative ability to shift times easily will be crucial to it.

Transcendent Present	Narrative Present	Major Flashback	Embedded Flashback	(Extra Time Level)

Chapter 1

9–11 The overview of the train running toward Port Warwick.

    11–15 Milton, Dolly, and Ella Swan arrive at the station.
       15–18 Milton and Helen meet and marry.

    18 Milton tries to stop time.

    18–20 Milton sits in the car while the hearse is repaired.
       20–23 Casper's visit the previous day to the Loftis house.

    23–24 Helen sits in her bedroom on the morning of the funeral.
       24–27 Milton's visit the night before to announce the death.

    27 Helen readies herself for the funeral.
       27–28 Helen begged by Milton to take him back.
          28–30 Peyton as a little girl wants to see the bees.
       30–31 Milton calling up pleasant memories for Helen.
          31–32 The loving moments of their early marriage.
       32 Milton begs to stay the night with Helen.
32 Biblical quotation.

    32–37 Milton enters diner to read Peyton's last letter.
       37–39 Peyton's recount of her breakup with Harry.
    39 Milton talks with Hazel, the waitress.

Transcendent Present	Narrative Present	Major Flashback	Embedded Flashback	(Extra Time Level)

Chapter 2

40–46 Milton reflects on his father while the hearse is repaired.

    46–54 Sunday morning when Peyton is nine; Dolly's cigarette burns.
    54–55 3 P.M. that afternoon; Dolly and Pookie visit.

        54–56 Milton phones Dolly that morning.

    56–60 Friction with Helen over Dolly.

    60–63 Milton and Dolly flirting; Peyton and Buster hurt Maudie.

    63–67 Peyton's apology.

Chapter 3

68–70 Dolly reflects that Milton now will leave her forever.
    70–77 Previous afternoon, Peyton's death revealed at club.

    77–83 Peyton's sixteenth birthday party; she is caught drinking.

    83–90 Helen tries to make Peyton go home.

    90–96 Milton says Peyton can stay.

    96–98 Milton and Dolly make love in the golf museum.

    98–102 Charlie LaFarge kisses Peyton.

102–4 Funeral cortege passes Daddy Faith's contingent.

Chapter 4

105–9 Carey Carr, driving to Helen's, debates what to say to her.
    109–11 Recalls her first visit to him in 1939.
        111–12 Recalls Adrienne's rumors about Milton.
    112–14 Helen begins her story of trouble.
        114–19 Helen's first hatred of Peyton.
    119–20 Carey consoles Helen.
        120–26 Peyton allows Maudie to fall.
    126–28 Carey and Helen talk of finding God.

Transcendent Present	Narrative Present	Major Flashback	Embedded Flashback	(Extra Time Level)
				128–34 Helen paranoid, her world breaking up.
				134–40 Helen confronts Dolly at the Bide-a-Wee.
	140–41 Carey still debating what he will say to Helen.			
		141–43 Other visits from Helen, tries to straighten her out.		
	144 Carey arrives.			
	144–49 LaRuth advises Helen to take Milton back.			

Chapter 5

Transcendent Present	Narrative Present	Major Flashback	Embedded Flashback	(Extra Time Level)
	150–52 Hearse gives more trouble; Milton will not talk to Dolly.			
		152–55 Nov. 1942, Milton considers futility of marriage.		
			155–73 Christmas 1941, Helen and Peyton argue.	
			173–75 Subsequent events, the affair with Dolly.	
		175–88 November 1942, Dolly beginning to resent Peyton.		
		188–94 Milton goes to the Charlottesville hospital, Maudie ill.		
			194–95 Milton's first "experience" with Audrey.	
		195–97 Milton meets Hubert in hospital, go to KA house.		
		197–201 The fraternity party, Milton seeks Peyton.		
		201–6 Milton insults Pookie and his girlfriend at cafe.		
		206–10 The football game.		
		210–12 Milton, having fallen into culvert, arrives at party.		
		212–16 Tells Peyton of Maudie's deteriorating condition.		
		216–18 They wait in the hospital corridor.		
			218–24 Maudie and Bennie.	

Transcendent Present	Narrative Present	Major Flashback	Embedded Flashback	(Extra Time Level)
		224–25 Helen vents her frustration on Milton and Peyton.		
		225–27 Peyton and Dick Cartwright speeding in car.		
			227–32 Cartwright's background.	
		232–36 Cartwright "takes" Peyton at his home.		

Chapter 6

237–46 Carey and Helen catch up with funeral cortege, he consoles Milton.

246–51 Calm period between Maudie's death and Peyton's wedding.

251–53 Night before Peyton's arrival for wedding.

253–56 Milton surrenders identity to Helen.

256 Happiness on the eve of the wedding.

256–59 Rejection of Dolly, vacation with Helen.

259–60 Milton's feeling of rejuvenation.

260–69 Milton and Peyton drink and talk prior to wedding.

269–75 The wedding ceremony.

275–86 Milton misspeaks, LaRuth trails in hot dogs, etc.

286–89 Tension increases at the wedding reception.

289–90 Vision of Peyton as a child.

291 Milton feels his mood crumbling.

291–97 Helen furious over Peyton's treatment of Milton.

297–98 Helen dreams of Dolly's death.

298–99 Helen walking with Carey at reception.

299 Helen's vision of punishing Carey.

300–1 Helen's vow to "fix" Peyton.

301–5 Peyton breaks down to Doc Holcomb.

Transcendent Present	Narrative Present	Major Flashback	Embedded Flashback	(Extra Time Level)
			305–14 Helen assaults Peyton, Milton goes to Dolly's.	
314 Overview of the ferry addressed to "you" (as the opening pages were).				
		314–22 Peyton and Harry await the ferry.		
		322–24 Dolly reflects outside while others are in the chapel.		

Chapter 7

325–28 A general history of Potter's Fields, in New York and elsewhere.

328 Police discover Peyton's body.

328–33 The courtship of Harry and Peyton.

333–34 Harry and Lenny identify the body.

335 Biblical quotation.

335–86 Peyton's last day—interior monologue.

387–89 Milton begs to have Helen back; scorned; attempts to strangle her.

389–99 Daddy Faith preaches to the Negroes.

399–400 The baptism.

The more simplified structure of *Lie Down in Darkness* is immediately apparent. First, the Transcendent Present time level is very infrequently and less purposefully used. As opposed to Stingo's employment of it to reveal his research and constructively analyze the meaning of the events he has been recounting, here we get only the sense of historical flux, the indication of a cosmic and universal backdrop against which all of this is taking place. Trains thunder blindly and predictably down the tracks, others have died and wound up in potter's fields and so forth. In contrast with the other three novels, one wonders if it is even needed here—the Transcendent Present is always an intrusive time level in Styron, though here the purpose of it is more questionable.

Furthermore, the chapters themselves are very regularly constructed, with the possible exception of the final one. Most open in the Narrative Present and finish there as well, not so of *Sophie's Choice*. Chapters Two and Five never make the return to the present, although the next chapter places the reader there immediately nonetheless. In every chapter the Major Flashback is in solid control of the full effect, and those flashbacks, as we have seen, are essentially chronologically ordered:

1. Peyton as a little girl.
2. Milton and Dolly become aware of each other, when Peyton is nine.
3. Peyton's sixteenth birthday, when the Milton-Dolly affair begins.
4. The commencement of Helen's visits to Carey Carr.
5. The events in Charlottesville, Peyton at twenty-one, when Maudie dies.
6. Peyton's wedding.
7. Peyton's suicide.

Never does the Narrative Present attempt to challenge the drama of the Major Flashback, for the former gives the sense of things irrevocably done (Milton's despair and exhaustion), while the latter seems always to be driving toward impending climax, both in themselves and in terms of their individual contributions to the final tragedy of suicide and disillusionment. In *Sophie's Choice* we have a Narrative Present which is equally as dramatic as the Major Flashbacks, and even in *The Confessions of Nat Turner* we get more of a sense of things needing to be reconciled, answered, settled before Nat's execution, even though Nat in his Narrative Present is chained in his cell. When Milton Loftis finally lunges at Helen's throat in the final pages of *Lie Down in Darkness*, there is the sense of anticlimax about his action, of gratuitousness. Whereas Nat comes to a Narrative Present epiphany that he was incapable of having in the past (i.e., in the flashbacks), surely Milton has learned nothing new, at least about Helen. His actions seem terribly melodramatic.

What makes *Sophie's Choice*, then, in the long run a more powerful book is Styron's artistic decision to write two fully-formed plots—the Stingo-Sophie-Nathan encounters of the Narrative Present and the Sophie-Holocaust story of the Flashbacks—which dramatically collide with one another in such a way as to give the past *active* meaning in the present and so the ability to redirect it in a Bergsonian sense. In *Lie Down in Darkness* the Narrative Present resembles an automobile accident victim lying in traction trying to figure out what hit him and his own role in his terminal paralysis.

We might note here that Styron began *The Way of the Warrior*, alias "Marriott, the Marine," very much the same as he did *Sophie's Choice*—apparently there was ultimately to be a strong Narrative Present as well as the typically powerful Major Flashback which has always been characteristic of Styron. According to Styron's interviews on the subject, the present will involve the narrator's new understandings of himself and the Marines (one, Marriott, in particular) while the Flashbacks will deal with an atrocity in which the same marine was involved in the past.[16] Since both novels were begun in the late 1960s or early 1970s, the similarity of method is not surprising, nor is it surprising either given the fact that Styron had already demonstrated an inclination toward a two-plot framework in *The Confessions of Nat Turner*. Not that he fully achieved it there, and probably he did not fully seek it; but the dynamism between Nat and Gray and also Nat and his soul is much greater that that of Peter Leverett and Cass Kinsolving reflecting back on their days in Sambuco.

I would like now to examine the structure of *Nat Turner*.

Transcendent Present	Narrative Present	Major Flashback	Embedded Flashback

Part One

3–5 The vision of the house on the promontory.
    5–12 Nat in his cell on the day of the trial.
        12–28 Nat's first interview with Lawyer Gray.
    28–41 Nat and Gray go over his confession.
        41–75 Judge Cobb's visit the day Hark is baited.
    75–87 The trial and theories of Negro inferiority.
        87 Nat's recollection of Margaret's school tale.
    88 Gray drones on at the trial.
        88–93 Nat and Margaret speak of poetry and other things.
    93–95 Discussion of evolutionary theories.
        95–105 Richard Whitehead's sermon; Nat's thoughts of revolt.

Transcendent Present	Narrative Present	Major Flashback	Embedded Flashback
		105–15 Sentencing, discussion with Hark, Nat refused a Bible by Gray.	

Part Two

Transcendent Present	Narrative Present	Major Flashback	Embedded Flashback
		119–28 Nat demonstrates his ability to spell to the guests.	
	128–29 Nat summarizes his memories as he awaits death.		
		129–30 Nat's grandmother on the auction block.	
		130–32 Nat's visit, at thirteen, to his grandmother's grave.	
		132–33 How Nat's mother became a house nigger.	
		133–34 Nat asks who his father is.	
			134–35 Story of his father's flight.
		135 Nat is told his father is in Pennsylvania.	
		135–38 The ten-hole privy.	
		138–40 The dullness of being a nigger child.	
			140–42 Nat's first interest in books at six or seven.
		142–50 Nat and his book while McBride rapes his mother.	
		150–54 Little Morning turns him in for stealing a book.	
	154–56 Reflection on Fortune and its directions—the results of the book stealing.		
		156–57 Nell and Louisa teach Nat to read.	
		157–66 Visit of ministers to inquire about slavery attitudes.	
		166–75 Nat made *special* in all respects.	
		175–83 Encounters Miss Emeline in the bushes.	
		183–201 Samuel Turner's promise of freedom.	
		201–8 Willis.	
		208–16 Nat accidentally delivers Willis for sale.	

Transcendent Present	Narrative Present	Major Flashback	Embedded Flashback
		216–21 Samuel Turner castigates himself for the sale of Willis.	
		221–28 Turner sells off everything and everyone.	
		228–38 Nat waits alone for Reverend Eppes.	
		238–45 Nat works for Eppes as a "slave."	
		245–47 Nat sold by Eppes, kindles his hatred for Turner.	
		247–52 Moores buy Nat, whip him for reading.	
252 Nat recalls Gray asking what God ever said to him.			
		252–53 Hears God say "I abide" in Moore's wagon.	

Part Three

Transcendent Present	Narrative Present	Major Flashback	Embedded Flashback
257–59 Analysis of Negro hatred of the white man.			
		259–67 The Northern white woman frightened by Arnold.	
		267–76 Summary of the years with Thomas Moore.	
		276–77 Hark separated from his family.	
			277–86 Hark's escape toward Pennsylvania.
		286–92 Nat's dream vision of the angel in 1826.	
		292–99 Free nigger Isham curses Moore.	
		299–311 At Nathaniel Francis's, Nat begins preaching freedom.	
		312–20 Nat "saves" Ethelred T. Brantley.	
		320–28 Nat steals map, works for Mrs. Whitehead.	
		328–30 The battle plan.	
		330–36 Nat assembles his inner circle of four.	
		336–40 Margaret, undressed, in the library.	

Transcendent Present	Narrative Present	Major Flashback	Embedded Flashback
		340–48 Nat's "signs"—the eclipse and the shot.	
		348–52 Nat outlines the battle plan to the four lieutenants.	
		352–53 Hark's resolve to kill.	
		353–74 Will's flight and the last conversation with Margaret.	
		374–91 The battle commences, Nat's failure to kill.	
	391–93 Gray's narration of some of the failures.		
			393 The girl who escaped to spread the alarm.
	394–98 Gray narrates more failures.		
			398–402 Other Negroes resist their efforts.
	402–3 Nat's vow to do it all again, the same way.		
		403–15 Will's challenge, the killing of Margaret.	
		415–17 Nat allows the Harris girl to escape with the alarm.	

Part Four

Transcendent Present	Narrative Present	Major Flashback	Embedded Flashback
	421–22 The vision of the white house on the promontory.		
		422–24 Nat talks to Hark through the wall.	
		424 Nat wakes to see the sun rise.	
	424–26 Gray brings Nat a Bible.		
426 Masturbatory fantasy of Margaret Whitehead.			
		426–27 Hark taken away to be executed.	
		427–28 Nat taken away to be executed.	
429 Two epigraphs.			

Except for the indications that Styron is becoming more interested in developing a more dynamic plot line in the Narrative Present, this is perhaps Styron's least complexly-structured novel.

Virtually everything happens in the Major Flashback level, and only three times in the entire novel does he descend to the Embedded Flashback time level, which is totally uncharacteristic of the other three works. Although this might be correctly written off to the fact that Styron was heightening the intensity of the Narrative Present and simply paying less attention to the level of deep reflection, it probably has more to do with Nat's own statement of the essential dullness of Negro existence in those times. To have dynamic associations one must have dynamic memories, for repetition tends to deaden rather than enliven the mind. It is doubtful that most of the other slaves would have been able to retreat even to the Major Flashback level for, unless they had particularly tragic experiences such as Hark did, there would be little out of the ordinary to recollect. The present would dominate because the present is yesterday, today, and tomorrow all compacted.

Nat, on the other hand, *is* special—he has a lot of memories which are quite different from what the other Negroes could have. They are fully-structured scenes, however, and are usually free of the attendant associations which "free" people might be able to bring to their most meaningful memories. Put another way, Nat deals in bold colors—memories of sexual initiation, of realization of bondage, of awareness of his "difference," of excruciating disappointment, of lust and love, of war. He would not be likely to attach associative memories which explore the shadings of guilt, nihilism, and metaphysical despair. His experience of life, until his final reflective period in jail, simply has not been had on such cranial levels. Such are the "luxuries" of the physically comfortable.

On the three occasions when Nat's story does enter the Embedded Flashback time level, there is significant similarity among them. One involves his father's flight to Pennyslvania, another Hark's foiled attempt to get to Pennsylvania himself. The remaining one is Nat's own early "escape" into books from the dullness and pain of Negro slave existence. All three are stark contrasts to the life he daily experiences and consequently easily recollects.

Not only does the story line rarely shift to the Embedded Flashback, it only very infrequently undergoes a time shift back to either of the present levels. When this does occur, the emphasis seems to be on the ironic contrast between promise and realization once again. In Part One, the scene in which Nat goes over his trumped up confession with Gray is shifted into the day he experienced compassion from Judge Cobb. Later, while Gray drones on in tedious legalese, Nat calls up the memory of his reading poetry with Margaret Whitehead. When he hears that the Negro is less evolved than the white man, he reflects on Richard Whitehead's vacuous and pig-headed sermons. Late in Part III, Gray's enumeration of the revolt's collapse sends Nat into recollections of why in fact it *did* collapse, an answer Gray has not the slightest suspicion of: that Nat purposely allowed the Harris girl to spread the alarm in order to exorcise his new-found guilt over the murder of Margaret Whitehead.

Other than this, the narrative confines itself almost entirely to the well-shaped scenes of the Major Flashbacks. The use of the Transcendent Present in this novel, though done sparingly, demonstrates Styron's passage from the impersonal, universal voice of *Lie Down in Darkness* to the knowing, analytical, thoroughly-versed voice of the later Stingo—Nat's statements on Fortune and its ironic workings, his discussion of black hatred for the white man, and his mythic visions of the white house on the promontory. Again, however, I do not think that Styron's use of the Transcendent Present ever became truly effective in thematic terms until he created the "older" Stingo behind the younger one in *Sophie's Choice*. Only then did that voice and that time level seem to justify themselves simply because, for the first time, they became a long-after-the-fact analysis of his own learning process—the "Araby" voice I mentioned earlier.

Finally, let us turn to the ambitious, if not entirely successful, structuring attempt in *Set This House on Fire*. This novel, following on the heels of a highly-admired first novel and a critically-acclaimed novella, demonstrates all the ambitiousness (and self-indulgence) that such notoriety can easily invite.

Transcendent Present	Narrative Present	Major Flashback	Embedded Flashback

Chapter 1

3–7 Peter summarizes his recent visit to Carolina to visit Cass Kinsolving.
    7–17 Letter from Cass and Peter's visit with his father.

Transcendent Present	Narrative Present	Major Flashback	Embedded Flashback

17–18 Recollection of his near-drowning as a boy.

18–19 Wires Cass that he is coming the next day.

19–36 Peter's departure from Rome, the car accident.

36–46 First meeting with Cass and Poppy at accident scene.

Chapter 2

47–56 Cass tries not to answer Peter's questions about Mason Flagg.

56–70 Peter meets Mason, Rosemarie, and Saverio.

70–72 Peter dozes in the Hotel Bella Vista.
72–93 Mason, Wendy, and his thirteen-year-old mistress.

93–103 Peter's entrance into Mason's Party.

103–22 Peter and Cripps confront the drunks.

122–24 Flagg pursues the girl past Peter.

124 Peter reflects on this memory; the Polaroid camera analogy.

Chapter 3

125–31 Peter and Cass in North Carolina speak of evil and Greek tragedy.
131–37 Peter meets Mason in New York City, late 1940s, before Europe.
137–38 Mason's tale of espionage training.

138 Peter encourages Mason to amplify.
138–40 Mason and the fourteen-year-old Yugoslav girl.

140 Peter gullible "four years before Sambuco."
140–42 Mason's escape from Yugoslavia.

142–45 Peter meets Celia while Mason is in bed with Carole.

145–48 Mason and Peter, in New York City, discuss the death of art.

148–49 Peter's recollection of the two mental photos.
149–52 Mason shows Peter his erotica.

152–53 The two mental photos again.

Transcendent Present	Narrative Present	Major Flashback	Embedded Flashback
		153–56 The orgy.	
		156–65 Last day before sailing—Peter and Celia.	
		165–74 Peter and Mason part on the *Queen Mary*.	
Chapter 4			
		175–92 Mason disgraces Cass in late hours at Sambuco.	
		192–215 Cass steals the medicine and tends Michele.	
		215–28 Francesca found ravished and Mason dead.	
		228–32 Departure of movie crew from Sambuco.	
		232–41 Cass returns after being missing all day.	
Chapter 5			
	245–49 Cass admits he killed Mason and that Mason did not rape Francesca.		
		249–59 Cass orders Poppy and children out of Paris flat.	
	259 Transition into Cass's diversion.		
			259–65 Vernelle Satterfield in Wilmington, N.C.
		265–78 Cass wanders Paris, resolves to move south.	
Chapter 6			
		279–85 Cass Stops drinking, becomes anti-American.	
		285–91 Peggy's sickness in Toulon.	
		291–96 Cass's self-deprecating diary.	
		296–312 Card game with McCabes and its aftermath.	
Chapter 7			
		313–33 Cass discovers Sambuco, arrested for disorderliness.	
		333–61 Kinsolvings move to Sambuco, hire Francesca.	
		361–64 Cass's journal, reflection on Slotkin and love.	
Chapter 8			
		365–66 Sketch of Waldo Kasz.	

Transcendent Present	Narrative Present	Major Flashback	Embedded Flashback
		366–68 Cass's dream of the black girl on the plane.	
	368–70 Peter and Cass discuss their attitude toward Negroes.		
			370–78 Cass and Lonnie wreck Crawfoot's house.
	378–79 Cass analyzes the Lonnie incident.		
		379–98 Mason thinks Cass is Kasz.	
		398–402 The liquor bottle with which Mason "owns" Cass.	
Chapter 9			
		403–15 Cass and Mason drive to the Naples PX.	
			415–22 How Cass became Michele's doctor.
		422–31 Cass disgraces himself in PX.	
Chapter 10			
		432–33 Cass and Peter tear down the long shut walls of his recollection.	
		433–46 Cass searches for drugs, finds Francesca in fright.	
			446–47 Cass's vision of American girls.
		448–65 Francesca ravished, Cass pursues and kills Mason.	
		465–77 Police investigation, Luigi lies for Cass.	
		477 Cass goes to buy liquor.	
	477–78 Cass tells Peter of a murderer's emotions.		
		478–94 Cass near American villa, with priest, in jail.	
			494–97 Luigi's tale of British bombers.
		497–99 Luigi's apology for lying.	
		499–501 Cass's return to Poppy after his ordeal.	
Epilogue			
	505–7 Letters to Peter from Cass and from Italian nun.		

As usual the body of the story takes place in the Major Flashback time level, but Styron handles that level differently from the novel which preceded it and the two which follow. Here that time level involves only two days, two very intense days to be sure, in which Peter Leverett wrecks his car, nearly kills a local in the process, sees his long time "friend" Mason Flagg murdered, a girl fatally ravished, and a dypsomaniac suffer the ultimate consequences of his affliction. The Major Flashback level in *Nat Turner* involved about a quarter of a century, in *Lie Down in Darkness* about the same, in *Sophie's Choice* about a decade. Hence the emphasis in *Set This House on Fire* is not so much on the course of time and history and its effect upon individual lives as it is upon the sensational interaction of disparate personalities on the very occasion when those personalities cannot help but become fully activated. The two-day period is so intense, in fact, that it virtually needs no higher time levels to give it meaning. The Embedded Flashbacks, which would be simple flashbacks without the complex time structure, could easily have supplied the context, the meaning, and the rationale of the story.

The Transcendent Present is so infrequently employed as to be pointless, I think. Except for the opening three pages in which Leverett sets the context of his recent visit to South Carolina and conversation with Cass Kinsolving, and the "Epilogue" in which he receives the two letters which tie the story up, the novel reverts to this time level only three other times. All of these occur within one thirty-page stretch in Chapters Two and Three, and all three involve the unnecessary "Polaroid photo" image Peter uses to distinguish between what appears to be the case versus what really is or at least may be. These occasions are so limited and ultimately inconsequential that the reader may miss them; but, typical of the Styron narrative pattern, this time level is present as usual.

More bothersome is the Narrative Present which does rather obtrusively recur in the story, at least through the first half of it. As Cass and Peter fish together, they attempt to tear down "the walls which had long shut in his [Cass's] recollection." (*SHF*, 433) For me this device fails in this novel because less is at stake in the

Narrative Present than in Styron's other three: Nat is about to be executed, Milton Loftis has somehow contributed to his daughter's ruin, Stingo is watching his two best friends destroy themselves. In the present novel Cass has already gotten control of his existence by the time the Narrative Present begins, and Leverett has little more cause than bad dreams and idle voyeurism to open up the Sambuco incident with him. There is little drama on the banks of this Carolina stream, and Styron almost has to remind himself to drop in there periodically. Less than five percent of the entire narration take place on that level, and two-thirds of that occurs in the first three chapters. In the last seven chapters this time level is evoked for a page or less at a time on a half-dozen occasions, often with 125 or so pages intervening. The level not only has no drama, it virtually evaporates.

I would like to draw several conclusions about the evolution of Styron's narrative technique, offering *Sophie's Choice* once again as his fullest and most perfect realization of his aims. First, he clearly prefers a first person mode, though he probably moved to it one novel too soon. *Lie Down in Darkness* required the third person if we were to have such scenes as the Helen-Carey and Peyton-Harry relationships in dynamic action. *Set This House on Fire* uses a first person narrator, but to no particular effect—it is a third-person story in which the first-person narrator can never seem to find a role for himself. Clearly *Nat Turner* and *Sophie's Choice* employ powerfully involved, epiphany-gaining narrators who are critically involved.

Second, Styron was clearly in search of some use for the Transcendent Present time level, but he located no sufficient function for it until his latest book. I think he learned the technique from Warren—he admits to admiring the opening pages of *All the King's Men* in *Sophie's Choice*—but he told *Lie Down in Darkness* in the third person, which gave Jack Burden's convincing reveries to *no* identifiable voice. He established voices in his next two novels, although neither one had any particular constructive use for the Transcendent Present. Finally, Stingo did in what I have called the

"Araby" voice—he told a complex story which meant something quite different in the Transcendent Present of thirty years later than it did in the Narrative Present of 1947.

What I am concluding on this point, then, is that *Lie Down in Darkness* needed three time levels instead of four, *Set This House on Fire* two instead of four, *Nat Turner* three instead of four. Only *Sophie's Choice* required all four, and it was there that Styron found the sort of fictional art he strives for appropriate to subject and theme. "Marriott, the Marine" seems to suggest that he will repeat the process in *The Way of the Warrior*.

Third, Styron's evolving narrative structure was closely connected to the themes he was establishing as well. If his ultimate statement concerns what Steiner called "time relation" and I have extended as "Transfer," then the ability to shift one's consciousness among a wide variety of people, places, and times becomes critical. It is the main escape from our Solitary visions which emphasize the brutal disparity between promise and realization in our own existences and cause us to force Fortune without any sense of guilt. The ability to view the world from a multitude of perspectives is the major curative for this in Styron.

Fourth, and closely related to the third conclusion, is the Bergsonian analogy I drew earlier in this chapter, or even the Marcel analogy if one prefers Cheshire's. The way to human freedom and out of psychological determinism (Bergson) or to human control and out of "ontological disorientation" (Marcel) is through effective and unifying understanding of time and memory. The four time levels tie in with this effectively. The Narrative Present is the level on which the parasitic self and ontological disorientation are realized. The memory searches into the predominant recollections of its past, examines those for their pregnant but hidden meanings (Major Flashbacks) and almost magnetizes related associations to them (Embedded Flashbacks) which clarify what those major memories really amount to. (For example, in Chapter Eight of *Set This House on Fire* Peter and Cass are reflecting on the nature of evil in the story's Narrative Present. Mason and the two days in Sambuco form the Major Flashback which suggests itself for examination. Yet, attached to these memories of Mason and Francesca is the

Embedded Flashback association of the day Cass and Lonnie point-lessly wrecked an old Negro's shack. Such a memory broadens the understanding of Evil and of mankind and, suddenly, of Cass him-self who perpetrated much the same sort of evil more or less as a lark in his idle hours.) Finally the Transcendent Present is that moment which all of us aspire to when, in the not too distant future, we will be able to "understand" what human existence is and, pref-erably, should be.

In each of Styron's novels the Transcendent Present is aspired to, although only in *Sophie's Choice* is it really attained. Only in that novel does the voice in that time level—the elder Stingo's voice—stake claim to some greater insight (gained from his memories of Sophie, her stories of the Holocaust, and his younger self) and demand that the rest of the human race, first, recognize what he has learned and, second, be on with extending its vision beyond Stingo's own abilities to see. The three narrators of the earlier novels come on with less certainty and, as a result, the full possibilities of the Styron narrative structure are not fully realized. In *Sophie's Choice* they are; form and theme have merged into a unified whole.

Notes

1. Ardner R. Cheshire, Jr., "The Recollective Structure of *The Confessions of Nat Turner*," *The Southern Review*, 12 (1976), 110–21.

2. Cheshire, p. 110–11.

3. Cheshire, p. 111.

4. Cheshire, p. 111.

5. Cheshire, p. 118.

6. Cheshire, p. 120.

7. Cheshire, p. 121.

8. Cheshire, p. 111.

9. Shiv K. Kumar, *Bergson and the Stream of Consciousness Novel* (New York: New York University Press, 1962) is a valuable piece of scholarship dealing with Bergsonian influences on modern narrative techniques.

10. Henri Bergson, *Matter and Memory*, trans. Nancy M. Paul and W. Scott Palmer (London: Allen and Unwin, 1962), p. 128.

11. *Mississippi Quarterly*, 17 (1963–64), 9–20.

12. Klotz, p. 15.

13. Klotz, p. 17.

14. The theme and narrative structure of William Golding's *Free Fall* are somewhat similar. See John K. Crane, "William Golding: The Free Fall of Free Will," *Bulletin of the Rocky Mountain Language Association*, 26 (1972), 136–41.

15. The gaps between sets of page numbers on the following four charts indicate that Styron himself broke the page in his novel at this point. Where there are no gaps, the time shifts occur with no visible indicator other than the instructions given by the narrative itself.

16. In the interview with Michiko Kakutani (cf. Chap. 6, n.l), Kakutani summarizes Styron's words on *The Way of the Warrior* this way: "Animated by such familiar Styron preoccupations as evil, guilt and domination, the novel is somewhat reminiscent of Conrad's *Lord Jim*. It focuses on the spiritual plight of a brave and intellectually gifted Marine colonel who is obsessed by the memories of an atrocity he committed in Nicaragua years before. The book, says Mr. Styron, is intended to be a kind of 'parable of the United States' nosy involvement in places like Latin America' " (p. 26). [Professor James L. W. West III of Virginia Polytechnic Institute and State University has lately informed me, however, of yet another change in Styron's thinking about this projected work. I quote Professor West: "Styron's present plan (the last time I talked to him) was to take that material and split it into two novellas, write a third novella dealing with Stingo's trip to Trieste on a cattle boat, and publish the whole in one volume as a series of three novellas about Stingo."]

INDEX

165

The Root of All Evil

THE ROOT

THE THEMATIC UNITY OF